FOCUS ON MARK

a study guide for
groups & individuals

revised edition

by
Robert L. Schwenk

Formerly published as *Focus on the Gospel of Mark*.

LIVING THE GOOD NEWS
a division of The Morehouse Group
Editorial Offices
600 Grant, Suite 400
Denver, CO 80203

Cover and interior design and composition: Polly Christensen

The scripture quotations contained herein are from the New Revised Standard Version Bible, copyright © 1989 by the Division of Christian Education of the National Council of the Churches of Christ, in the USA. Used by permission.

ISBN 1-889108-68-5

Contents

Introduction to the Focus Series

THE FOCUS BIBLE STUDY SERIES offers a unique and inviting way to interact with and experience God's word, allowing that word to filter into every area of life. It is designed to challenge growing Christians to explore scripture and expand their understanding of God's call. Each volume echos the **Living the Good News** strategy of experiential learning; that is, they welcome the participant into a journey of discovery.

Journal Format

Focus Bible Studies are adaptable for individual use or group use. Adult classes, small-faith communities, midweek Bible studies and neighborhood discussion groups will find these books a helpful resource for in-depth exploration, personal growth and community building. When used in a group, leadership may be designated or shared.

Each of the book's twelve sections begins with a brief synopsis of the passage and a *Find the Facts* section, which can help you prepare to consider the material. Informative commentary is not intended to provide definitive answers to the meaning of the passage, but to give you background information, clues to the context and suggestions for thought. It can serve as a point of departure for personal reflection or group discussion.

The questions posed in each section are designed to engage the reader at a variety of levels:

- Some are questions of *interpretation:* What is the author's meaning in this passage?

- Some are questions of *application:* How does the author's message apply to contemporary Christianity?

- Some are questions of *reflection:* How is this God's message to me? to my family? to our community?

Every level contributes to the faith-nurturing impact of the study. The variety of questions are grouped together topically so that you can respond to the level most directly pertaining to your situation. The same goes for group use: participants can respond to those questions most relevant to their current circumstance.

Each section includes suggested *Group Activities*. These activities provide small groups with experiential activities that can help participants to grasp an idea through various methods of learning rather than through intellect alone. These activities involve the whole person—senses, emotions, mind and spirit. If you are using this study in a group setting, we encourage you to incorporate these activities into your group's time together. Many adults may feel awkward when invited to work with clay or pipe cleaners, or to create songs or poetry; they may feel these are childish activities. Such concrete experiences, however, can serve to move group members from learning *about* an idea toward an *understanding* of the idea.

Each section closes with a *Journal Meditation* and a *Stepstone to Prayer*. These offer you the opportunity to record or illustrate thoughts and feelings about the passage explored and to express these to God in prayer. The *Journal Meditation* invites you into deep, personal reflection that can produce life-changing understanding. *Stepstone to Prayer* leads you into a time of communion with God.

Individual Use

- Begin each session with prayer—that you will be open to God's message to you, that the Spirit will illuminate God's work, and that you will be empowered to follow God's call.

- Read the passage several times in the scripture translation of your choice. (Note that the New Revised Standard Version Bible has been used in the preparation of these studies.) Try to understand what the author is saying before you begin to interpret, apply or reflect on the message.

- Note key words or phrases that you find especially significant in the scripture. When you have finished a section, go back and review these words or phrases and explore their importance in light of your greater understanding of the passage.

- Spread your exploration of any given section over several days; come back to those question that have provoked considerable thought. You may be surprised at the new insights you find if you spend some time each day on the passage. Give the passage time to sink into your heart and mind.

- Record your thoughts in the space provided. The discipline of journaling can help you synthesize your thoughts and direct your understanding.

Small Group Use

- Prepare for each gathering following the suggestions given above under "Individual Use." Group interaction is impoverished if participants have not immersed themselves in the passage before meeting.

- Begin your time together with prayer. Expect God to increase your faith, expand your understanding of scripture and build your fellowship.

- Accept one another's experiences and interpretations of the passage. Listen carefully to comments; offer your own insights; be willing to look at things in new ways.

Small Group Leadership

- Prepare for each gathering as a participant first. Your role as a leader is not to teach but to facilitate the process of sharing and discovery for everyone.

- Keep in mind the group's time restraints. Begin and end on time. Underline those questions that you think will be most appropriate for your group's discussion time, but be open to those questions that group members wish to pursue.

- Choose one or two group activities that your group will enjoy and learn from. Make sure you have gathered any required materials for your chosen group activities.

- Begin and close each gathering with prayer. Ask a volunteer to read each section of the passage as you come to it in the study.

- Welcome all contributions, but keep the discussion on track. Certain passages may have two or three possible interpretations. Do not be concerned if all participants do not agree in their understanding. Acknowledge the differences of opinion and move on to the next question.

- Allow time at the end of each gathering for those individuals who wish to share their thoughts or drawings from their *Journal Meditations.*

- If your group members are not well-acquainted, it may take some time to build trust within the group. Let the dynamics of the group develop as group members gain confidence in themselves and in one another.

Introduction to the Gospel of Mark

The Gospel of Mark *moves*. Mark plunges headlong into the ministry of Jesus—no fancy introduction, no opening theology, no Christmas story. The action is fast and furious, with events tumbling on each other's heels. "Immediately, immediately, immediately" repeats Mark in his opening verses. The time is now; the message has come. Mark pulls his readers into the healing, teaching, delivering ministry of Jesus.

The Jesus of Mark's gospel is a man of action, healing diseases, stilling storms, feeding crowds, exorcising demons, forgiving sins, leaving behind a trail of amazed believers and dazed opponents. In this gospel, Jesus seldom stops long to preach or teach; another village beckons, another hurting believer cries out for healing, every morning brings a fresh opportunity to serve.

The Gospel of Mark is the shortest, simplest and most concise of the gospels. In Mark we find the "basic gospel," possibly honed and sharpened to be used in catechesis in the early Church. Understandably, then, a large percentage of the gospel—over a third—covers the critical events of the final week of Jesus' life. These events stand at the heart of Christian faith and life.

Author and Date

The author of the Gospel of Mark cannot be identified with certainty. As with the other gospels, the book itself offers no identification. However, both early Church tradition and selected verses from the New Testament suggest a likely candidate—a man by the name of John Mark.

Acts refers to John Mark as the son of Mary, a woman within whose house the early Church met in Jerusalem (ACTS 12:12). John Mark appears again in COLOSSIANS 4:10, identified as the cousin of Barnabas.

Both Barnabas and John Mark travel with Paul on his first missionary journey to Cyprus and Galatia. For unknown reasons, Paul and Mark have a falling out and Mark leaves part way through the trip. The fight is serious enough so that even Barnabas declines to join Paul on his second tour when Paul refuses to allow Mark to accompany them again.

Mark appears later in the New Testament in letters written by Paul from prison in Rome. By this time the wound between them has healed; Paul refers to Mark as his "fellow worker" (PHILEM. 24) and "useful in my ministry" (2 TIM. 4:11). Mark apparently ministers to Paul while Paul is imprisoned.

Mark's appearance in Rome toward the end of Paul's known ministry also links Mark to the apostle Peter. Tradition places both Peter and Mark ministering together in Rome while Paul writes from a Roman prison. Mark, it is thought, remembered and organized the sermons of Peter, arranging them into what is now known as the Gospel of Mark. Thus, a more appropriate title for the book could be "Peter's Gospel." A comparison of the structure of Mark with the sermons of Peter in Acts lends credence to this theory; Peter's typical sermon and Mark's gospel begin with John's baptism and end with the resurrection. Mark presents the "basic gospel" in his book just as Peter presented the "basic gospel" each time he preached.

Although filled with strong Jewish elements, the Gospel of Mark focuses on Gentile believers as its target audience. For example, Mark takes time to explain Jewish customs and translates Aramaic words already familiar to Jews. Mark stresses the need to bear up beneath persecution and martyrdom, relevant matters for Roman believers toward the end of the first century.

Much has been invested in the attempt to date Mark's gospel. Many scholars see Mark's gospel as the precursor to those of Matthew and Luke, with whom Mark shares a great deal of material. If Matthew and Luke relied on the recollections of Peter as recorded by Mark, the

Gospel of Mark probably dates from A.D. 50–65. Other scholars theorize that all three gospel writers relied on one or more other, unidentified sources. Mark may then be dated a decade or so later, from A.D. 60–70. The evidence in this matter remains inconclusive. In either case, the Gospel of Mark would have been read and reread by many people who had witnessed firsthand the events he describes.

Structure

Here is a simple outline of the Gospel of Mark:

MARK 1:1-13 —Jesus' ministry begins.

MARK 1:14–9:50 —Jesus ministers in and around Galilee.

MARK 10:1-52 —Jesus journeys to Jerusalem.

MARK 11:1–13:37 —Jesus ministers in Jerusalem.

MARK 14:1–15:37 —Jesus suffers and dies.

MARK 16:1-20 —Jesus rises to new life.

Themes

The Gospel of Mark presents Jesus as the suffering servant, ready to face persecution, rejection and alienation to obey his heavenly Father. And those who follow Jesus—those who aspire to discipleship—must also suffer for his sake and the sake of others. "Who will be greatest?" ask the disciples. "The one who is a slave to the others," answers Jesus. And more clearly than in any of the other gospels, Jesus carries that teaching to its ultimate expression. "For the Son of Man came not to be served but to serve, and to give his life a ransom for many" (10:45).

The cross figures prominently in Mark's gospel. Mark takes pains to balance both the human contribution to and the divine need for Jesus' death on the cross. MARK 14:1 offers an example of human involvement in the crucifixion: "The chief priests and the scribes were looking for a way to arrest Jesus by stealth and kill him..." MARK 8:31 offers an example of God's intention: "Then he began to teach them that the Son of Man must undergo great suffering, and be rejected by the elders, the chief priests, and the scribes, and be killed, and after three days rise again." God prepares Jesus to die on the cross; humanity nails him there.

Mark also carefully balances the humanity and the divinity of Jesus. Of all the gospels, Mark offers the most emotional and human picture of Christ. In Mark more than the other gospels, Jesus is moved, filled with compassion, tired out, amazed, touched and angered. In stories where Luke and Matthew soften Jesus' human side, Mark describes Jesus in terms that we might use to describe ourselves; for example, in Mark the Holy Spirit "drives" Jesus into the wilderness (1:12) while in Matthew the Spirit "leads" Jesus (4:1). Despite these frequent references to Jesus' humanity, Mark also points out Jesus' divinity—unclean spirits worship Jesus (3:11; 5:7), God calls Jesus the Son (9:7), and Jesus refers to himself as the Father's Son (13:32).

Though Mark focuses less on Jesus' teaching and more on action, as noted above, he does not neglect the importance of Jesus' teaching ministry. Mark applies the words *teacher*, *teach* or *teaching* to Jesus nearly forty times. While fewer of Jesus' actual teachings are recorded, Jesus is clearly recognized as a remarkable teacher.

Mark also tends to shroud Jesus' role as the Messiah in secrecy, waiting for the final week of Jesus' life to announce Jesus' identity as the Christ. For example, just prior to the final journey to Jerusalem, Jesus tells his followers not to tell anyone what they had seen until he had risen from the dead (9:9).

This, then, is the Gospel of Mark: fast-paced, detailed, essential. Mark invites us to join the march and walk with Jesus, the Messiah. We watch as Jesus heals, listen as he teaches, struggle side-by-side with him in the quest for wholeness and love, endure persecution and opposition, and, finally, join him at the cross as he purchases our salvation. Welcome to Mark, the gospel of Jesus Christ, the Son of God.

Mark 1
The Way of the Lord

JOHN THE BAPTIST BURSTS ON THE SCENE after the prophetic voice in Israel had been silent for four hundred years. He challenges his people to prepare a way in their hearts in the same way that people in the Orient made the road smooth for a visiting king. John urges the people to take away the barriers and the rough places, and to make the way of the Lord a smooth entrance. This is not a one-time preparation but a continual readiness and maintenance program. John the Baptist calls for a spiritual discovery: a tough-minded awareness of our failure to measure up to God's will and a radical change of heart, determining to follow God's will more closely.

Moving through the first days of Jesus' ministry in chapter 1, we see the forces that the Lord will encounter when he comes on the path into our hearts. There will be religious objections, resistance to change, family resentments, emotional distress and physical symptoms that erect huge barriers to the coming of the Lord.

Read through all of the book at one sitting, if possible. This creates the sense of drama and awe that Mark wishes to communicate. Then reread MARK 1.

Find The Facts

What prophet does Mark quote? What does John preach? What does John say about Jesus? What does Jesus preach? Whom does Jesus call to be his disciples? What examples of Jesus' power does Mark include? How does Jesus teach? What does Jesus say is the reason he came?

Consider:

1. List the kinds of people, powers and attitudes that Jesus encounters in the first chapter. What contemporary name can you give to each of them?

2. Note the word immediately wherever you find it in the text. What impression do you think Mark wishes to create? Why?

3. Read Isaiah 40:1-11. Compare Isaiah's message with John's. What more can be understood about John's message and Jesus' identity from Isaiah?

Mark 1:1-8

John cries out, announcing the arrival of the Messiah. John's ministry is one of preparation, calling people to repentance, baptism, confession and forgiveness—the elements of our own preparation for encountering the living God. There is no other way than this "repentance road" on which the King is able to enter the hearts of his people. Confession and forgiveness remove the barriers that obstruct the King's embrace of love.

To *baptize*, (Gk., *baptizo*) literally means "to dip in" or "immerse," implying also "to wash clean." John invites the people of Israel to be cleansed from sin by repentance, turning away from old ways and moving in the opposite direction.

Confession, which means "to agree with someone else," involves the open acknowledgment of the truth about our sin—to ourselves, to God and perhaps to another person. Confession specifically names the offensive behavior, recognizes its darkness and brings a disciplined effort to turn away from it. John hears the people's confessions before the people are immersed in the water. He searches their attitudes and questions their behavior (Lk. 3:7-17). This verbalizing is the outward show of their repentance, which makes them candidates for baptism. Confession does more than recognize sin; it agrees with God about sin's seriousness.

John's attire and lifestyle clearly indicate his role, for they echo Elijah's protest against the superficial and materialistic lives of his contemporaries (2 Kg. 1:7-8). Though John attracts many by his powerful message, he has come not to gather people to himself but to "prepare the way of the Lord" (Jn. 1:19-27). Jesus far surpasses John, as John certainly recognizes. Only the lowest of slaves would remove a person's sandals, one of the most menial and humble of tasks.

4. *Using your own words, list in order those steps that must be taken to meet with the Lord. Name and agree with God about one attitude or behavior that needs to be changed in you. Go through the steps you have just outlined.*

5. *Do you think John consciously associates himself with the prophets who came before him? Why or why not? What other messages might John wish to communicate through his lifestyle? What does John's lifestyle suggest about his freedom from the values or opinions of those around him?*

6. *What differences and similarities do you see between John's water baptism and Jesus' Holy Spirit baptism? Read John 3:1-8. How does Jesus' conversation with Nicodemus further explain the two baptisms?*

Mark 1:9-13

Jesus' arrival at John's place of ministry signals the beginning of his own ministry. As the people seek God, Jesus joins them in an act of complete identification. He goes down into the Jordan with these admitted sinners and submits to the same baptism. Though he has no need for repentance or forgiveness, the first step in his mission of atonement (2 COR. 5:21) involves the decision to associate himself fully with the human condition (MT. 3:15).

This act leads first to affirmation from God; it expresses perfectly Jesus' identity as God's Son. It also leads to a time of severe testing, the narrow, spiritual pathway that continues the repentance road. Before Jesus can reach out effectively to others in their sin, illness and spiritual perversity, he first must face his own temptations to minister in ways other than his humble, loving, forgiving, suffering-with-others style.

Consider:

7. What does Jesus' baptism reveal about the nature of his ministry? In what ways does Jesus' baptism define his calling from God? What does our baptism reveal about our ministry and calling?

8. In what ways do you think God's voice and the descent of the Spirit prepare Jesus for his wilderness experience? What part do wilderness experiences play in maturing us as Christians?

Mark 1:14-20

Jesus' public ministry begins as he preaches the gospel (literally, "good news") of the nearness of God's kingdom. This kingdom is not some far-off place or event, but an open door through which any person may enter by repenting and believing. The time is ripe; the decisive moment (Gk., *kairos*) has begun a new epoch.

In this new season, Jesus invites people to move from the empty obedience of ceremonialism to a fellowship based on sacrificial love. Some hear this good news gladly and follow Jesus. The word *follow* literally means to "walk the same road." It implies fellowship, joint-participation and a side-by-side experience with another. Jesus' leadership is not one of distant direction, but of intimate sharing in the joys and trials of a common path. That path, however, transforms those who walk on it. Following Jesus entails submitting to his revolutionary call.

Consider:

9. *Why do you think Jesus chooses these four men as his first disciples? What qualifications do they have? What qualifications do they lack? On what basis do we often accept or reject fellow disciples?*

10. Are all Christians called to be "fishers of men"? Why or why not? To what other parts of the fishing-for-people enterprise might you be called? setting the sail? steering? washing the nets and decks? throwing the net? What does this passage say about the way we become Jesus' disciples?

Mark 1:21-28

Capernaum stood at the crossroads of a key caravan route at the northern end of Lake Galilee. In the synagogue of this busy town, people gathered for prayer, praise and the reading and interpretation of scripture. The Greek indicates that Jesus teaches at some length, and his teaching is like being "struck hard by a fist." The people are utterly amazed by what Jesus says and the way he says it. He teaches with authority, unlike the scribes who teach by quoting a tangle of regulations made by other rabbis. Jesus explains the inner law of the Spirit based on compassion and human worth.

Mark juxtaposes the power of Jesus' words with the power of Jesus' works. Jesus first displays this power and compassion to a man with an unclean spirit in a place of worship and teaching. One wonders what this man was like before Jesus' teaching and what there is about Jesus that brings this spirit out into the open.

In Jesus' day people quickly recognized the reality and power of evil spirits and demons. Strange and aberrant behavior, pathological and some physical illnesses were considered a result of evil spiritual powers. The earth was a frightening place, a hell, where every life situation was ruled by these demonic spirits. Archaeologists have uncovered thousands of skulls with holes drilled in them that show growth after the drilling. Such drilling was thought to release evil spirits from the head. Jesus' authority over this demon amazes the people, for only God has control in this dark arena.

Consider:

11. For what reasons might the first event of Jesus' public ministry and the first display of resistance have happened in a synagogue? What might this say about Jesus' work today?

12. What is the significance of a demon's recognition of Jesus? of Jesus' response to the demon? What words today are sometimes used to refer to demon possession?

13. *What does Mark imply about the scribes' teaching? How does Jesus' teaching differ from contemporary preaching and teaching?*

Mark 1:29-39

Here, at the beginning of history's central event—the advent of Jesus Christ—Mark records the healing of a mother-in-law. Mark sandwiches this event between the exorcising of a demon in the midst of Jewish worship and huge crowds bringing other demon-possessed and physically ill people. Peter's mother-in-law shows the proper response to Jesus' touch: service prompted by gratitude and devotion.

What Jesus has done in the synagogue spreads like a firestorm. The people could hardly wait for the Sabbath to end, as signaled by the first three visible stars. So at sunset, a flood of people come to Jesus, carrying or leading their sick, confused and maimed friends and family members. With compassion and power Jesus responds. Many can speak with a semblance of power, but few are able to follow through with deeds of power. Jesus produces results.

After telling of the first busy day of Jesus' ministry, Mark now shows us the secret of Jesus' effectiveness—solitude and prayer. In his baptism, Jesus identifies with people who are aware of their separation from God and who desire to return. Only Jesus' consistent, personal, spiritual practice of spending hours alone with the Father can sustain him in his mission of identification and atonement.

After the time of quiet, Jesus is ready to abandon the immediate adulation of the crowds (1:37) in order to fulfill his greater calling. Everyone indeed is searching for Jesus.

14. Compare today's Church members to the crowds that were attracted to Jesus. How would you characterize Jesus' style of ministry? How might this be adapted to your church's ministry in the world?

15. Describe your spiritual practice. Name your lonely place. In what ways does the time you spend with God prepare and empower you for service?

16. What do you think Jesus' followers want him to do in verse 37? Why? What form do you think this voice takes in the Church today? What kind of confidence enables Jesus to leave the success at Capernaum?

Mark 1:40-45

The Greek word for *leprosy* does not necessarily mean the disease we now identify by that name (also known as Hansen's Disease). A variety of skin diseases went by the name "leprosy" and were the most dreaded of all diseases.

In ancient cultures, illnesses and misfortune were seen as a punishment from God and/or the work of evil powers. Such affliction was believed to be a result of the sin committed by the sufferer or his or her parents. The terror of leprosy lay in the diminished physical changes that inevitably came and in the social and spiritual rejection associated with it. The leper lived apart from the community and, when encountering other people, yelled out "Unclean! Unclean!" so that others could avoid contact. Worst of all, no leper could participate in worship or join the community in any religious activities. No one had less dignity or hope than a leper.

By calling out for help, coming close and kneeling at Jesus' feet, this leper breaks the law. When Jesus reaches out and touches him, he, too, breaks the Levitical law. Jesus obeys instead the higher law of a compassionate heart. By cleansing this man's disease, Jesus reconciles the leper to his community and to God. The priest's declaration of ritual cleanliness reinstates the outcast in his family and in the society. The theologically trained scribes wonder how Jesus can supersede God's wrath and punishment (3:22, 30).

Consider:

17. *What faith and doubt does the leper experience? How is this like your own faith and doubt?*

18. *How does the leper benefit by showing himself to the priest? How does the community benefit? What might this say about the ministry goals of the Church today?*

Group Activities

1. Divide into groups of three and invite group members to share the event and circumstances of their own baptisms. Encourage them to tell about the location, their age, social circumstances and personal meaning of the event. Discuss:
   - How does your baptism compare with Jesus' baptism?

2. Dramatize Jesus' wilderness temptation. Invite people to roleplay *Jesus, the Holy Spirit, Satan, the wild beasts* and *the angels.* Read 1:9-13 phrase by phrase and let the roleplayers express what they imagine and feel. Dramatize and discuss any insights that came to them.

3. Review MARK 1 and ask group members to cite the various encounters that Jesus is having with people. List them on chalkboard, whiteboard or newsprint. Discuss:
   - Who takes the initiative in each situation?
   - What is the outcome of each situation?

   Divide into groups, asking each group to choose a situation from this passage to present as a "frozen frame." Ask them to discuss privately the encounter that they wish to dramatize without words or movement, frozen as in a still photograph. Have the groups watch each presentation and guess which encounter is being depicted. Discuss:

- What is the effect on you of Mark's clipped and hurried style of telling Jesus' story?
- In what ways does focusing on Jesus' individual encounters enhance or detract from Mark's overall account in this passage?

4. Invite group members to brainstorm some human conditions and taboos that cause people to be as ostracized and feel as unacceptable as lepers did in Jesus' day. Discuss:
- When have you felt like a leper?
- Who or what are we expected not to touch?
- Name a taboo that your compassion has caused you to break.
- What groups today are treated like lepers (e.g., AIDS victims)?

Journal Meditation

For a moment close your eyes and imagine a road that stretches out before you for miles. It is a rough road, with hills and gullies, dangerous barriers and deep holes. God is coming to you down this road, but is having a difficult time reaching you. Let the Holy Spirit show you the road hazards of your life. What must you remove? What must you level and fill in? What crooked places need to be straightened out? What must be bridged in order to prepare the way of the Lord? After a few minutes of quiet meditation, write down or illustrate what has occurred to you.

Stepstone to Prayer

Lord, if you are willing, you can make me...

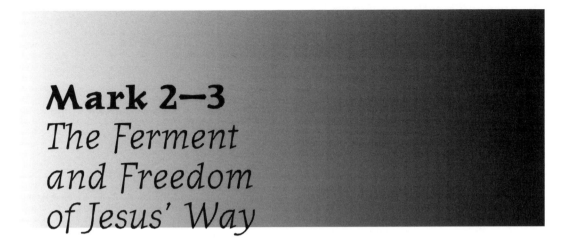

Mark 2–3
The Ferment and Freedom of Jesus' Way

JESUS' MESSAGE AND HIS ACTIONS BRING HIM INTO CONFLICT with the religious, economic and political leadership of his nation. His way causes such ferment that none of the existing social structures and mores can contain the effects of its transformative power. The freedom of choice that his Spirit-led faith sets loose is too threatening to the keepers of the status quo.

In these chapters, Jesus takes on the prerogatives of God by healing and forgiving what others thought to be punishment from God for sin. Jesus' forgiveness breaks through religious limits with an explosive freedom. Those who cling to rigid rules of religiosity must oppose Jesus or lose the foundation on which they have built their philosophy and safeguarded their privileges and power.

Read MARK 2–3 carefully before answering the following questions.

Find the Facts

Whom did Jesus heal? What religious law did Jesus allegedly break in each healing? Whom did Jesus call to follow him? Where did the scribes say that Jesus got his power? Who are Jesus' mother and sisters and brothers? What special mission did Jesus have for the Twelve? Whom did Jesus come to call?

Consider:

1. In chapter 2, Jesus repeatedly shatters the religious expectations of those around him. Read through Jesus' responses in verses 8-11, 17, 19-22 and 25-28. What do you think Jesus is saying about his source of authority? his new way of spirituality?

2. Consider the different stories that Mark includes in chapters 2 and 3. What do you think Mark most wants to communicate about Jesus?

Mark 2:1-12

Jesus' home in Capernaum became the base for his early preaching ministry. The word translated *preaching* refers more specifically to simple conversation than dramatic speech. The power of Jesus' message was not in the presentation but in the proclamation of truth that cut through barriers.

Jesus' response to the persistence of the four stretcher bearers confounded everyone. The four men brought their friend for healing, and the crowd apparently expected another miracle (1:32-34). Jesus offers a greater gift: forgiveness.

The Greek word for *forgive* implies letting go and leaving behind a burden. By imparting forgiveness, Jesus reassures the paralytic that God has let his sins drop and wishes to go on in a new relationship untainted by the failures of the man's earlier life. Jesus' words imply that the man, too, must now let go of his old ways to walk anew in God's way.

Many first-century Jews believed that serious physical ailments probably were God's punishment for some serious transgression of the law (JN. 9:1-2). Jesus neither refutes nor affirms this belief, but moves the focus away from the cause of the man's dilemma and on to Jesus' mission as the Son of man, God's chosen representative. Jesus' actions presume a unique relationship with God. Not only can he forgive sin, thus spiritually restoring the man, but he can demonstrate his authority with visible physical restoration.

Consider:

3. Whom do you know who is helpless, who cannot get up and do anything about a paralyzing situation in his or her life? How can we carry such people to Jesus today? When have you been the one lying powerless on a pallet? Upon whose faith have you relied?

4. How do you answer Jesus' question in 2:9? When have you experienced Jesus' power in forgiveness and healing?

5. What seemed to provoke Jesus' declaration of forgiveness? What does this passage say to you about the importance of community in our spiritual journey?

Mark 2:13-17

Here Jesus again reaches out to a "sinner." Levi was a tax collector for Herod Antipas. He had probably paid a high price for this powerful position and was becoming rich by charging the caravans more tax than the government demanded and pocketing the difference. The people despised tax collectors for betraying them and entering into state-supported crime and injustice (Lk. 19:1-10). It took a tough-minded, bold, aggressive person to be so completely independent of other people's disapproval. Levi apparently loved money and power more than the respect and approval of his fellow Jews. He had "guts" that matched his greed.

Yet Jesus sees Levi's need for healing and knows that, when Levi has let go of the burden of his lust for money, he will be free to follow Jesus.

To follow means to walk the same road. This was neither an invitation nor a suggestion, but a command. To follow Jesus involved a total commitment to his authority and a participation in his experiences (8:34).

In first-century Jewish culture, the most intimate moment with a friend was at the dinner table where, over a leisurely meal of many courses, quiet conversation was shared. To invite a man to dinner and to accept it was a witness of acceptance and friendship. No Jew who cared about appearing righteous had close associations with "sinners," those who rejected their interpretation of the law.

Consider:

6. *Who in your community is on an unacceptable-to-eat-with list? Why? In what ways do you follow Jesus' example of unprejudiced friendship?*

7. *Levi was an unlikely choice for a disciple of Jesus. Who do you know who is just as improbable a candidate for discipleship? What does Jesus' initiative say about the nature and power of evangelism?*

8. *What do you think Jesus is suggesting in verse 17 about the true nature of righteousness? Read Luke 18:9-14. In what ways do "sinners" today need to humble themselves to hear Jesus' call?*

Mark 2:18-22

The strictest Jews set aside two days a week for fasting. The tax collectors did not observe these disciplines, and on this occasion neither did Jesus. Yet the law also made provisions for setting aside regular fasting in favor of celebrations like weddings. Thus it recognized that different occasions merited different attitudes and behavior.

Here Jesus points out that the joy of his presence, like the joy of a wedding, overrides the solemnity of the regular fast. It would again be appropriate to fast when "the bridegroom is taken away from them"; that would be a time of sadness, loneliness and longing. But for now, what others perceived as a time for sorrow, Jesus calls a time of celebration. Jesus' new way calls for an inner sensitivity to God that has a higher priority than ritual. His actions teach that ritual, tradition and self-discipline can help to nurture a relationship with God, but they cannot make the relationship possible.

By naming himself the bridegroom, Jesus may have been recalling the Old Testament theme of the marital relationship between God and Israel (Is. 54:5; 62:5; Jer. 3:14, 20; Hos. 2:16). This theme recurs in the reflections of other New Testament writers and becomes a key to understanding the relationship between Christ and the Church (Eph. 5:22-32; Rev. 19:7; 21:2, 9).

Jesus illustrates his new way with a short parable. New cloth sewn on an old garment will shrink, thus causing a larger tear. New wine expands as it ferments; used animal skins, which have already stretched as much as they can, will burst. In the same way, the old customs of the law cannot contain the power and freedom of Jesus' new way.

Consider:

9. Why did John's disciples fast? Why did Jesus' disciples celebrate? What roles do fasting and celebration play in your spiritual life? When do you conform to your understanding of God's will for you rather than others' expectations? with what consequences?

10. Name one spiritual desire, feeling or need fermenting within you that cannot be expressed through your present spiritual structures or traditions. What old wineskins might God be calling you to discard? What alternatives for new wineskins do you have?

11. *Consider some of the controversial issues facing the Church and society today (e.g., abortion, human sexuality, violence, etc.) in light of Jesus' words in 2:21-22. In what ways does Jesus' teaching give contemporary Christians guidance as they seek to apply his principles to contemporary life?*

Mark 2:23—3:6

Jesus immediately demonstrates this new freedom. Among the Pharisees, the Sabbath, with its blessings of rest, worship and quiet, had been turned into a rigid routine full of regulations and restrictions.

While Jesus does God's work on the Sabbath, his disciples feel free to strip heads of grain off their stems to strengthen their sagging energies. The Pharisees, self-proclaimed protectors of the rules for goodness, keep harping on this as a violation of the "no work" prescription for the Sabbath.

But Jesus justifies their actions on the simple basis that they are hungry, like David and his men who ate the consecrated loaves of the tabernacle (1 SAM. 21:1-6). They are free to keep the spirit of the Sabbath—physical and spiritual renewal—though they break the rigid interpretations of the law. Thus Jesus demonstrates from their own scripture that there are times when higher demands supersede very good and normal patterns.

When Jesus enters the synagogue to worship—itself a pattern of obedience—he again overturns the old understanding of the role of the Sabbath by healing the man with a withered hand. Jesus demonstrates that the true meaning of the Sabbath—indeed, of all the law—is found in acts of compassion and restoration (Mt. 22:34-40).

Consider:

12. Read Deuteronomy 5:12-15 and Exodus 20:8-11. How is something kept holy? Is physical need a higher priority to be met than the maintenance of good worship ritual? Why or why not? (See Mt. 4:1-11.)

13. Why do you think Jesus felt anger and grief when the Pharisees would not answer him in the synagogue? What is "hardness of heart"? What did the Pharisees love more than the compassion of God? Why?

Mark 3:7-35

In verses 7-12, Mark describes Jesus' growing popularity among people from every corner of Palestine. Jesus is pressed on all sides by demands for healing and by confrontations with evil spirits. He chooses special disciples to train in order to expand God's ministry. Each disciple has a family history and a present career out of which his ministry will grow into its own unique expression of the gospel.

As Jesus continues his work, it becomes clear to everyone that his actions are extraordinary. Some conclude that he is possessed by satanic power. The name *Beelzebul* came from the title *Baal-Zebub*, which in Hebrew meant "lord of flies." This title was a derisive play on the name *Baal-Zebul*, which meant "lord Baal." Baal was a god of the Canaanite people of Palestine. The name Beelzebul was eventually used in reference to Satan, the "ruler of the demons" (MT. 12:24). Jesus points out the absurdity of their argument and proceeds to warn them of the spiritual dangers inherent in such false accusations.

Blasphemy against the Holy Spirit, slandering God by maliciously rejecting God's truth, hardens the human heart and shuts off the voice of God. When an ego is so well-defended that it must deny truth or deny the power of God's Spirit in Jesus so that it can maintain its status quo, that person is in a dangerous place. George MacDonald phrased Jesus' meaning well: "The one thing that cannot be forgiven is the sin of choosing to be evil, of refusing deliverance. It is impossible to forgive that sin. It would be to take part in it. To side with wrong against right, with murder against life, cannot be forgiven."

Talk of Jesus' claims and miraculous work reach his "mother and brothers," who now come to fetch him and restrain his wild talk (3:21). They may have expected him to be home giving leadership to his family. Instead he is creating dangerous controversy both by his radical teaching and his astonishing works. Jesus' new way redefines family loyalty both for him and for all of his followers.

Jesus' first loyalty is to his heavenly Father's will and to those who do that will. Once again Jesus rejects the traditions and the expectations of his day. By his radical commitment, Jesus shows that for those who follow him, there is no higher loyalty than to God's call. Love for families and the need for their love often compete with serious discipleship and its life-defining pathway.

Consider:

14. According to Jesus' response to the scribes, what proves that his activity is not generated by satanic power? What do you think the unclean spirits' knowledge about Jesus indicates (3:11)? What conclusions do you reach about Jesus' power over Satan?

15. In your own words, define the "unforgivable sin." When have you been tempted to believe that obedience and sacrifice for Christ were crazy, unnecessary, perhaps evil? What assures you that Jesus is filled with God's Spirit? that God's Spirit will also fill you?

16. *Read Matthew 10:34-39. Do you think blood relationships should always take second place to spiritual relationships in the family of God? Why or why not? What are the implications of such a rearrangement of loyalties? Where does the commandment to honor your father and mother fit in (Ex. 20:12)? When has your family misunderstood your goals or decisions?*

Group Activities

1. Read through MARK 2–3 again and list on a chalkboard, whiteboard or newsprint all the restrictions that Jesus breaks. Beside each of these, list a corresponding restriction in your community. Discuss:
   - What is the principle Jesus uses when making a decision about whether to follow the prescribed way or to break it?
   - How does this principle affect your list of contemporary taboos?

2. Reread the story of the paralytic and his four friends, MARK 2:1-12. Discuss:
   - The passage says nothing about the paralytic's faith and only mentions the faith of his four friends. When have you witnessed one person's faith operating on someone else's behalf?
   - In what ways might we offer our faith for others who are helpless? Consider contemporary crises in your community, your city, the nation and the world.
   - What does this passage say to you about prayer?

3. Reread the story of Jesus' healing of the leper, MARK 1:40-45, and compare it to the healing of the paralytic. List on chalkboard, whiteboard or newsprint

the common elements in the two stories. Discuss:

- How are the leper and the paralytic alike or unalike?
- To which character do you most relate? Why?
- What different aspects of Jesus does each story reveal?

4. Skim through the two chapters again for evidence of "hardness of heart" (3:5) in people's lives. List these on chalkboard, whiteboard or newsprint. Discuss together:

- Which of these are present in the Christian community today?
- What are some other contemporary symptoms of hardness of heart?
- What are some antidotes to hardness of heart?

Pray that the Lord would show you those ways in which you, like the Pharisees, harden your hearts against his way, and that he would open your spirits and minds to his healing touch.

Journal Meditation

Reread Mark 2:21. Consider areas in your life where you feel the most torn, where loyalties seem to be in painful conflict (e.g., relationships, children, time management, finances, goals, ambitions, etc.). List them in the space below. Now, beside each, list the ways you have tried to patch over the conflict. Is it working? Why or why not? Pray about each and wait for God to speak to you.

Stepstone to Prayer

Lord Jesus, lead me in your way...

Mark 4–5
The Ways of the Kingdom of God

IN THE FIRST PART OF THIS SECTION (4:1-34), Jesus begins to teach large crowds about the way the heavenly Father operates in the affairs and souls of men and women. He tells story after story using common, natural laws and human behavior to illustrate the unrecognized but active work of the Spirit. While this public ministry flourishes, he also begins to give his special followers the pattern for deeper discipleship. He invites this inner circle of friends to draw close to him as he further explains the ways of the kingdom.

In the second part of this section (4:35–5:43), Jesus begins to show the power of God's kingdom to create new life—both physical and spiritual. This divine power is made available by faith, a radical realignment of belief systems that results in victory over the chaotic forces of this world.

Read MARK 4–5.

Find the Facts

What images does Jesus use to describe the kingdom of God? In the parable of the sower, on what four kinds of soil did the seed fall? List the four miracles that Mark recounts in 4:35–5:43. Which people asked

Jesus to leave their neighborhood? How was the bleeding woman healed? What did Jesus say to the dead child?

Consider:

1. *Which parable in chapter 4 most closely describes your experience of God's kingdom? Why?*

2. *Which miracle in 4:35–5:43 would you have most liked to witness? Why?*

Mark 4:1-12

Jesus carefully avoids lecturing to the people, for he understands that the truth of God cannot be grasped by the intellect alone. His method of teaching involves simple storytelling. Such parables—stories that illustrate a deeper message—are designed not to conceal his meaning, but to illuminate the divine truths within human experience.

Jesus' first story in chapter 4, often called "the parable of the sower and the seed," is more truly a parable of the four soils. Every farmer in his audience was familiar with the problems of seed lost to birds, rocky soil and the ever-present weeds. Every farmer hoped for the abundant crop offered in the fourth soil that Jesus describes.

Jesus leaves the crowd with the story, inviting them to reflect on its spiritual truth. As he withdraws with his friends, he explains to them that the kingdom of God is a mystery, impossible to understand from the outside looking in. But when one is awakened to it through experience, then its presence and activity become clear. "Those outside" must come inside.

In verse 12, we see another mystery: the mystery of the blind and deaf soul. When Jesus speaks a parable that reaches past the intellect or beyond socially approved norms, and when the person hearing it has hardened his or her sensitivity to this deeper place, then the result—spiritual darkness—is both the choice of the person and the will of God. Sometimes God allows greater blindness in order to convince people of their complete inability to find their way. Jesus' parables invite them to explore God's way.

Consider:

3. Why do you think the kingdom of God is hidden from some? In what ways is it a mystery? Read Isaiah 6:9-10 and compare it with Jesus' words. Do you think Jesus' words contain any irony or sarcasm? Why or why not?

4. List every verb connected with the seed. What do these action words indicate about God's role and ours in evangelism?

5. List the characteristics of each kind of soil. Name the places in your life where these traits are present.

Mark 4:13-20

All the fields in Israel had pathways to and around them. Often they had been there for hundreds of years. These pathways were never intentionally watered or plowed, so seed lay on the surface until the birds ate them.

The pathway is the well-traveled way, the way most people walk. "Everybody's doing it" is the slogan of the hard-packed path. According to Jesus' story, the gospel has no hope of taking root in a heart hardened by the traffic of the world. Such a heart cooperates with the enemy, who robs it of new life.

The rocky soil refers to the thin layer of topsoil that covers much of the hardpan of Israel. Shallow-rooted grass for grazing animals grew in this area, but more deeply rooted plants could not live. The sun, heating the rock underlying this sparse earth, acted like an incubator so that the seed would spring to life more quickly. In spite of the quick beginning, the seeds could not thrive in this soil; the stress of the sun's heat dried them up from the roots and they would wither away.

In the same way, Jesus says, some people have an agreeable, receptive surface, but just below the surface lies a rock-hard resistance. Often hurts, fears and early traumas solidify into stony, hidden barriers, and when it becomes inconvenient or unpopular to cling to the truth, they fade away.

The thorny soil comments on the common practice of not thoroughly plowing or weeding a field. When the rains came and the new seed sprouted up, tender and green, the old thorns would quickly grow, choking out the new growth.

Here Jesus shows that well-established concerns, responsibilities, social distractions and economic security often leave no room for the new growth of God's concerns. When life is full of good things, the new priorities of the gospel, with its disciplines and goals, may easily be pushed aside and smothered.

What does it take to be good soil? It must accept the plow and have its life turned over and opened up. It must reject the well-traveled way of the world. It must be willing to uncover the hard-heartedness deep within, caused by present sin and past trauma. It must be ready to root out some good activities and concerns in order to make room for God's new ways in Christ. Only those who continue to grow and bear fruit truly walk in God's way.

6. Name some of the ways that the Church sows the word today. In what ways do you sow the word?

7. In what ways does Satan steal away the gospel today? When have you experienced such attempts to rob you of truth?

8. Name the most serious hurts you have ever received and the ways you defend yourself against further pain. In what ways do these defenses create hard places that resist God's grace?

9. What fruitfulness in your life leads you to believe that the word of God has indeed fallen on good soil in your life?

Mark 4:21-34

Again Jesus appeals to common sense in his teaching. The lamp's obvious purpose is to shed light in dark corners, to assist in uncovering and revealing. So Jesus comes, and his truth will inevitably penetrate all the hidden areas of our lives. The one who has "ears to hear" will welcome the light that dispels shadows. "The secret of the kingdom of God" (4:11) has long been a mystery, but now Jesus' teachings bring the truth out into the open for all who wish to receive it.

In verse 24, Jesus tells of a spiritual law at work that cannot be violated: the individual's response to the seed of the kingdom will determine the harvest he or she reaps. Failure to prepare the soil or rid it of rocks and weeds will mean famine when there could be a harvest. Generous care of the small seed of new life will result in a full crop.

After so emphasizing the responsibility of the hearer, Jesus offers two parables that show the paradox of the kingdom. On the one hand, we are responsible for the harvest; on the other hand, the seed has a life and destiny of its own that does not lie in our control.

For the two parables of new growth, we must visualize the methods of ancient farming. For the most part, Palestinian farmers were "dry" farmers, meaning they did not irrigate, but depended on rain for water. In these parables Jesus refers to the complete dependency of a farmer on the natural processes of the earth's fertility cycle. The words "he does not know how" are not just an admittance of ignorance but a confession of awe and wonder. The seed has within itself the sure and faithful power to fulfill itself. Wisdom, hope, faith and patience let things proceed at their own rate.

The small size of the mustard seed (4:30-32) shows that small beginnings are always God's way. Jesus warns his disciples to beware of the "big deal" and the glorious start. Even so he encourages them to respond fully to the call of the kingdom, for then these small beginnings will result in new life far more magnificent than the tiny appearance of the original act or thought

10. Compare the soil of the parable in 4:1-8 with the soil of the parable in 4:26-29. Who is ultimately responsible for the growth of the seed? How does this make you feel when you examine your own spiritual growth?

11. Read 1 Corinthians 2:6-14. In what ways does this passage help you understand Jesus' words in Mark 4:10-12 and 21-23? In what ways has the secret of God's kingdom been "disclosed" to you? In what ways does it remain hidden?

12. In what ways have you experienced the invincible growth of the kingdom of God in your own life? in the lives of those around you? in the life of your faith community?

Mark 4:35—5:20

Here Mark shifts his account from stories about the kingdom to real-life reports about the kingdom's power to changes lives. The two stories in this section must not be separated from one another, for they show two ways in which Jesus brings peace and calm to chaos. The first story tells of outer violence that results in an inner calm; the second story tells of inner turmoil that resolves into outer peace.

Lake Galilee's sudden storms descended from the frozen heights of Mount Hermon to the super-heated air of the Jordan valley. One would think that these men sailing with Jesus, some of whom were lifelong fishermen, had faced just about everything the lake could hand out. Yet they panicked, even with Jesus in their boat, even when Jesus had set their course and told them to go forth. In the face of their fear, Jesus quiets both the storm around them and the terror within them. Thus he demonstrates his absolute authority over creation and his complete reliability in situations that seem out of control.

The region of the Gerasenes was non-Jewish territory, so the possessed man may not have been Jewish. The man, a menace to his society, had been chained and finally banished to the dread and stench of the grave-yards, considered places of rampant evil-spirit activity.

A Roman legion was a regiment of six thousand soldiers. Here the term refers to the collective name of the many demons inhabiting the possessed man. The demons perceive Jesus' presence from afar and drive the man in fear to his knees before Jesus. They recognize Jesus' calm authority. Though they had wrought violence on the man and on all around him, their fierce and bloody ways immediately succumb to Jesus' words of power. Their only hope is to avoid banishment "into the abyss" (Lk. 8:31).

When Jesus brings freedom, some people do not welcome it. Instead of joy and thanksgiving to God for saving this man from his frenzied and angry life, the townspeople plead with Jesus to leave. They are most concerned about the sudden demise of their herd of pigs, their source of economic security. Fear or selfishness make them unwilling to become poorer for the sake of another less fortunate than themselves.

13. *Reread 4:40. Why does Jesus rebuke the disciples? In what did they lack faith? How do you think Jesus expected them to demonstrate their faith? What false expectations do you think the disciples had? When has this been true of you?*

14. *What kind of treatment had the possessed man received at the hands of the townspeople before Jesus arrived? How do we treat afflicted people in our community? How well do you think the Church communicates Jesus' authority and compassion?*

15. *What do the effects on the townspeople of Jesus' action say about the effectiveness of the Church's ministry in contemporary communities? Why do we see such little evidence of Jesus' power in the Church today? How do people today react to the work of the Church?*

16. *When do you, your family, your community or the Church choose to send Jesus away for economic and security reasons?*

Mark 5:21-43

As a ruler of a synagogue, Jairus organized the worship service and supervised administrative affairs. His request of Jesus is particularly striking because earlier Jesus' actions had antagonized the Pharisees (3:6), whose activities centered around the synagogue. Many Jewish leaders perceived Jesus as a threat to the accepted order of Jewish life.

Jairus, however, ignores the judgments of others. He and many other Jewish religious leaders refused to accept the conclusions of the hostile scribes, Pharisees and Sadducees (12:28-34; Lk. 20:39; Jn. 3:1-1). Jairus swallows his pride and, before a crowd of curious onlookers, begs for Jesus' intervention.

At this point Mark interrupts his tale to tell of a woman who, like Jairus, humbles herself before Jesus, hoping in the face of a hopeless situation. There is nothing more draining of physical, emotional and financial strength than a prolonged illness. This woman had used all her resources in countless painful and misguided medical procedures.

The flow of blood was not only a constant weakening of her strength and a great personal embarrassment, but it also placed her in the religious and social position of being unclean, that is, unacceptable for social company and worship events. One might think that Jesus would be put off by being her last resort, but he was not. Grace is surely amazing in its single-minded desire to heal and restore.

The thought of being healed by touching the hem of Jesus' garment seems superstitious. Perhaps she thought herself unworthy of his special attention or was afraid there would be a price tag attached. Whatever her reasons, the woman hoped to benefit anonymously from his powers. Jesus rewards her faith in spite of her misconceptions.

When Jesus wants to know who had touched him in this special, healing way, he shows her that she cannot take strength from Jesus without encountering him. There are no anonymous experiences with God. Grace is always a personal encounter, and so she came forth and told him everything.

The woman's interruption delayed Jesus just long enough to allow Jairus's daughter to die before Jesus could arrive. The mourning customs had begun with loud outcries of grief and sorrowful wailing. The people laughed at Jesus' unwarranted optimism. They knew death when they saw it. But Jesus and the little girl together had the last laugh. His word and touch restored her life, her strength and her appetite.

Consider:

17. Compare the emotions and attitudes of Jairus and the bleeding woman. What does this tell you about how we are to approach Christ? What do these two stories teach you about prayer? about faith? about grace?

18. How do you suppose Jairus felt when the bleeding woman delayed Jesus' arrival? When have you experienced similar feelings?

19. List the attitudes of those around Jairus before and after the death of his daughter. Then list Jesus' attitudes revealed in the story. When have you felt like Jairus's friends and neighbors? When, like Jesus, have you been able to ignore (5:36) the disbelief of others?

20. List the different ways that contemporary society offers freedom from suffering. Name the ways you have spent your strength and your abundance but have not been made whole or free. How can we touch Jesus' garment today?

21. How exactly was the woman healed? How important was Jesus' confrontation of the situation? How necessary was the woman's confession? In what ways does the desire to get something special from God motivate your spiritual life (prayer habits, devotional reading, liturgical involvement or standard of ethics)?

Group Activities

1. Before meeting, copy the following on chalkboard, whiteboard or newsprint: "The kingdom of God is like..."

   In the meeting, place a small plant, a piece of fruit and a large stone in the center of the group. Distribute paper and pens or pencils. Invite group members to write parables about the kingdom of God based on what they know about these objects. After allowing time for work, invite volunteers to read aloud their parables.

2. Invite group members to lie on the floor and close their eyes. Ask them to imagine that they are the earth and that they are looking up at a farmer who has come to sow his seed. The farmer casts the seed into the wind and the seed lands on them. While group members imagine this, read aloud the parable of the soils (4:3-9).

   Afterward, discuss:
   - What kind of soil were you? Why?
   - What does your soil need to bear an abundant crop? Where can you go for these resources?

3. On chalkboard, whiteboard or newsprint draw a large lake. Write *God's Kingdom* on one side and *The Kingdom of this World* on the other. Read aloud MARK 4:35. Invite group members to consider the following:
   - Just as Jesus invited his disciples to cross the lake, so he invites us to cross over into the kingdom of God. The disciples encountered a variety of obstacles, both external (wild wind and waves, physical inadequacies, etc.) and internal (terror, disbelief, feelings of abandonment, etc.). What obstacles, internal and external, do we encounter today in our journey into God's kingdom?

   List the ideas of group members in your drawing of the lake. Then distribute pencils and index cards. Invite group members to reflect quietly for a few moments on those obstacles peculiar to their personal experiences and write them on the cards.

   Close with a time of open prayer for faith and fearlessness.

Journal Meditation

Reread MARK 4:18-19 aloud. Take a few moments to consider the unfruitful areas of your life.

What are some of the "thorny" things in your life that choke the word? What "cares of the world" impede your spiritual growth? In what ways do you experience the "lure of wealth"? When does "the desire for other things" replace your desire for new life?

Consider changes in your life that might weed out some of these thorns. Record or illustrate your thoughts below.

Stepstone to Prayer

Lord, your word is present in me like the seed of new life. Help me to make room for its invincible growth by...

Mark 6
Expanding the Way of the Lord

BEGINNING IN CHAPTER 6, MARK'S STORY OF JESUS moves out beyond the familiar territory near the Lake of Galilee. The rejection of Jesus by his relatives and hometown neighbors from Nazareth propels him to offer the good news to others. His preaching missions will take him and his disciples into other Jewish towns and into the Gentile regions of Tyre and Sidon (7:24), Decapolis (7:31) and Caesarea Philippi (8:27). Those familiar with Jesus from his youth fail to receive his good news, but others who welcome his message are fed and filled by Jesus' compassion.

In this chapter, we read of many whose hearts are closed to God's work. They see but they do not perceive; they hear but they do not understand (4:12). Mark juxtaposes open-hearted individuals with close-minded skeptics as a warning and a call to faith for followers of Jesus in every age. Read MARK 6.

Find the Facts

Who takes offense at Jesus? Why? What does Jesus do after he sends his disciples on to Bethsaida? How much food was left over after the picnic? What message did the Twelve preach in the villages? Why did Herod imprison John the Baptist?

1. *From this chapter, what general observations can you make about Jesus—his mission, his character, his priorities? How would you describe his relationship with the Twelve?*

2. *Note Jesus' instructions for the disciples' training mission and their accomplishments (4:7-13, 30-32). How useful for the work of Christ in your community is the pattern of this mission? What applications can you see for the way we should do our work in the Church?*

Mark 6:1-6

Skepticism flourishes in Jesus' hometown. Why? Perhaps because of his teaching that cuts through old understandings. "He taught them as one having authority" (1:22); that is, he comes with a radical, new message that departed from the teaching that the people expect from the synagogue. Jesus' message always offends those who prefer old religious ways and refuse to risk by welcoming the new way of God's kingdom (Lk. 5:39).

Verse 3 gives another clue about the lack of acceptance in Nazareth, Jesus' hometown. "Is not this the carpenter...?" Clearly Jesus' neighbors had a certain expectation of Jesus' potential, which he exploded. What might this imply about the thirty years that Jesus had passed in this town? that he was a humble villager who never put on airs? who displayed no pompous pretensions? who could have been voted least likely to become famous and most likely to lead a quiet life of hard work and family loyalty? Perhaps. At any rate, the people gave him no honor and thereby forfeited his gifts of power.

Consider:

3. Compare Mark 6:5 with Matthew 13:58. Why does Mark seem to emphasize Jesus' inability to do many miracles in his hometown? What does this imply about the role of faith?

4. What are the implications of the eternal word of God being spoken and lived out in an untrained, sweaty carpenter, from a side street in a backwater town, who had lived in obscurity for 30 years?

Mark 6:7-13

This is a short learning mission. The directions and limitations placed on the disciples were applicable to later missions of the apostles and early believers, and for that matter, for followers of Jesus today, but we must understand that this is an example of controlled, "hands-on" learning, under conditions that demanded trust in God. The central goal was to extend Jesus' own mission.

Two by two is the Lord's way of training. Later the disciples may have enough confidence to launch out on lonely journeys for the sake of the gospel, but the basic pattern is partnership.

The support systems for these missions are to be meager or entirely lacking. Jesus deliberately places the disciples in situations of vulnerability, of dependence on resources outside of their control. Jesus asks the disciples to relinquish self-reliance and expect their audience to take some responsibility for salvation. Those who receive Jesus' followers receive Jesus himself; and those who receive Jesus, receive God (MT. 10:40; JN. 13:20). In offering typical generous Eastern hospitality, the people took the first step of repentance by hosting and welcoming the message of good news.

Those who refused to give hospitality closed the door to the good news. In shaking the dust off their feet, the disciples would declare that they had offered the message but that it had been willfully rejected.

The essence of the disciples' mission was threefold:

- to preach Jesus' message and call for repentance, i.e., for moral commitment and priority shifts

- to confront and exorcise evil spirits that possessed the hearts and minds of people

- to anoint with oil those physically ill, using the common medical and religious practice of the day, and to heal them

5. Reread Jesus' instructions to the disciples. What are some contemporary equivalents of the things they were to take and to leave behind? What are some contemporary equivalents of their tasks?

6. When have you been as vulnerable and exposed as these disciples? What did you learn? Under what conditions or for what purpose would you be willing to become this vulnerable again?

7. In what respects do you see your church being bogged down with supplies and equipment that might keep it from accomplishing the three aspects of the disciples' mission? What can you do about it?

8. Why do you suppose Jesus paired the disciples for their first mission on his behalf? What resources did partnership provide? In what ways does the Church today supply these resources?

Mark 6:14-29

When the disciples began to spread the word of Jesus, the authorities took notice. Herod, terrorized by his guilty conscience, believed that Jesus was John the Baptist returned from the dead. He was sure that Jesus had come to plague him for executing the prophet in order to save face with his friends and to appease the vengeance of his bitter wife. Herod knew that John was a "righteous and holy man." He wanted to protect the Baptist, but when his image as a powerful king was called into question, he abandoned his concerns for the Baptist's welfare to protect his reputation.

Others thought Jesus was the return of Elijah, who had been taken into heaven without death (2 Kg. 2:11). Through the prophet Malachi, God had promised to send Elijah to prepare the people for the day of the Lord (Mal. 4:5). No one, however, seems able to see Jesus for who he really is. Instead they try to fit him into a predetermined structure of truth that has no room for Jesus.

Consider:

9. Why did Herod and others need to explain Jesus as a returned spirit? What are some contemporary explanations of Jesus that fail to recognize his true identity?

10. What feelings and values motivated Herod to behead John when he respected him and wanted to preserve him? When have you sacrificed something important to you in order to gain approval from and power over others?

Mark 6:30-44

Jesus knows that a tough schedule leads to burnout, so he seeks a time and place where the disciples, after their training mission, can relax and rest (6:30-32). However, when they arrive at their retreat site, they find more work to do. Without rankle or resentment, Jesus teaches and ministers to the peoples' needs, spiritual and physical.

The importance of this miracle story cannot be overemphasized. It is the only miracle that all four gospel writers include in their accounts of Jesus' ministry. Mark tells us that the miracle was motivated primarily by compassion. He first satisfies their spiritual hunger (6:34) and then, much like his behavior in the story of the paralyzed man (2:1-12), meets their physical needs as well.

Which is easier: to fill up the empty souls of men, women and children, or to fill the stomachs of thousands of hungry people? The author of the Gospel of John more clearly addresses this question when he writes, in the context of this miracle, "Jesus said to them, 'I am the bread of life. Whoever comes to me will never be hungry, and whoever believes in me will never be thirsty'" (Jn. 6:35).

Consider:

11. *How does Jesus cope with the conflict between his desire for retreat and his compassion? When do you experience the same tension? What principle can you glean from Jesus' example? How realistic is this principle for your life?*

12. What does this story tell you about the tension between needs and resources? Consider your community's area of greatest need and the available resources. What principle can you apply from this story?

13. Read Exodus 16:2-15. Considering this event in Jewish history, what effect do you think the miraculous feeding had on the people?

Mark 6:45-56

Jesus decides to stay with the people after the meal and gives his disciples a head start across the lake. Then, after dismissing the crowd, he finds a lonely place and prays into the evening, while the disciples struggle to row against a strong wind. Sometime between 3 and 6 a.m., Jesus walks comfortably over the angry water, seemingly intent on letting the disciples toil while he goes on to meet them at the northern end of the lake.

Again his original plan is interrupted by his compassion (6:31-34); the disciples' fear and fight with the elements cause Jesus to turn aside and reassure them. His words to the disciples, "Take heart, it is I; do not be afraid," have surely comforted his disciples through the ages.

Consider:

14. *Why do you think it was important for the disciples to know that Jesus can walk over the rough water and calm the wind? What is the application in your life?*

15. *Reread 6:51-52. What connection do you see between the disciples' astonishment, their misunderstanding about the loaves and their hardened hearts?*

Group Activities

7:1 8:26

1. Make a list on chalkboard, whiteboard or newsprint of the most urgent needs in your community. Discuss together:
   - In what ways would the threefold aspect of the disciples' mission (6:12-13) meet these needs?
   - How would your community change if these three things were to take place regularly?

2. Discuss group members' responses to question 12 using the following steps:
   - Choose one large issue that your community now faces that is similar to the hunger crisis of the five thousand (6:35-44).
   - Decide together what resources would be needed, i.e., like the two hundred denarii of bread.
   - Write out what resources your group has, i.e., the five loaves and two fish.
   - Brainstorm ways that you can place your meager resources in Jesus' hands.

3. On chalkboard. whiteboard or newsprint, make three columns, labeling one *Herod*, the second *Herodias* and the third *John the Baptist*. Reread MARK 6:14-29 and list in each column the things that this passage says about each individual: his or her qualities (positive or negative), values, priorities, attitudes, etc. Discuss:
   - What one word would you use to describe Herod?
   - What one word would you use to describe Herodias?
   - What one word would you use to describe John the Baptist?
   - When have you felt like Herod? like Herodias? like John the Baptist?
   - Why does Jesus remind Herod of John the Baptist?
   - In what ways do John the Baptist's qualities listed in your chart apply to Jesus?
   - In what ways are these qualities present in your life?

Journal Meditation

Reread MARK 6:45-52. Let the story of the disciples being sent by Jesus across the lake become for you a personal blueprint of your present life situation. Describe below how and when you have been in a similar situation, trying to follow the direction of Christ with the wind blowing against you. How did you feel? Name the times when it felt like Jesus got into your boat, encouraged you and reduced the head wind.

Stepstone to Prayer

Soften my heart, Lord, that I may receive your miracles...

Mark 7:1–8:26
The Way of the Heart

THE FIVE STORIES IN THIS SECTION UNCOVER the building conflict between Jesus and the religious leaders of his day. He directly confronts the error of their teaching and then demonstrates his authority with several miracles. Yet he realizes that his words and works have set in motion the hostility that will ultimately lead to his death. To prevent an untimely confrontation, Jesus tries to work in secret, ministering quietly and privately to those who appeal to his mercy and compassion.

Here Jesus' way—a way of purity of heart—stands in stark contrast with the ways of tradition. Mark challenges disciples of every age to abandon their own ways for Jesus' way.

Read MARK 7:1–8:26.

Find The Facts

What were Jesus' disciples doing that offended the Pharisees? What was the traditional practice of the Pharisees? What example does Jesus give of the Pharisees' practice of neglecting God's commands in favor of their own traditions? Why does Jesus free the Greek woman's daughter? What miracles does Jesus perform in these two chapters? On a map, trace Jesus' travels in MARK 6:53–8:26.

1. *Carefully consider Mark's arrangement of these stories. Why do you think Mark uses this order? What progression do you see in the events?*

2. *Compare Jesus' attitude toward "the commandment of God" with his attitude toward "the tradition of the elders." What is the key to Jesus' way of making decisions about life?*

Mark 7:1-13

When speaking of "the law," Jews meant the first five books of the Old Testament in which were recorded the commands of God. Often obedience to these commands required wisdom and great moral discernment. To prevent transgression of the commandments, the Jewish leaders reduced God's principles for holy living into a tangle of rules and regulations to cover every possible situation. These human interpretations of divine laws had been handed down orally by teaching rabbis and were studied and meticulously monitored by the scribes and Pharisees.

Here Jesus points out the absurdity of such human definitions of the mind of God. In keeping their carefully delineated conditions for spirituality, they directly violated the intent of God. Ceremony invaded every area of life and drove true holiness far from their hearts. The keeping of the traditions made the condition of the heart irrelevant.

Jesus and his disciples do not follow the elaborate system of rituals and taboos that the most rigid of the Jews used. Jesus and his followers live like the common people, who had neither the time, the opportunity, nor, in some cases, the money to follow these rules.

The situations that Jesus addresses in this passage show the folly of these practices. The ceremonial washing neglected by Jesus' disciples provoked the criticism of the religious leaders from Jerusalem. But their rigid interpretation of "defilement" opens them up to Jesus' piercing condemnation of hypocritical traditions.

By devoting certain money "to God" (*Corban* means "an offering"), a man could get out of his obligations to care for his parents (Ex. 20:12) and then use the money for other purposes. Some scholars point out that the scribes rationalized this practice with NUMBERS 30:1-2, where Moses stresses the importance of a vow made to God.

Jesus redirects the issue by focusing on the intent of God's law: enabling God's people to live in harmony, to care for one another with compassion and, most importantly, to train them in loving God. Manipulating the law, by pitting one scriptural mandate against another in order to justify certain practices, fosters vain worship (7:7).

Consider:

3. *Read Isaiah 29:13. How does this verse describe religious hypocrisy? In what ways is the Church "teaching human precepts as doctrine" (7:7)? In what ways is your heart close to or far from God?*

4. Name one way in which you have given more attention to the appearance of something about your faith and the impression it makes than to the real truth in your heart. How can you change this situation to reflect more accurately true honor for God?

5. In what ways do contemporary Christians pit one scriptural mandate against another and end up violating the spirit of the law? What rules do you have that prevent you from caring for someone else?

Mark 7:14-23

Here Jesus returns to the Pharisees' first objection—the disciples' supposed defilement. Jesus shows that the rules of tradition kept the outside clean but could do nothing to contain all the evil things that come from within (7:23). According to the thinking in Jesus' day, an unclean or defiled person was out of relationship with God and therefore unqualified to receive God's blessings. Jesus shows that fellowship with God has nothing to do with the kind of food or drink consumed. The life God has created is good, not unclean, and therefore no dietary discipline makes fellowship with God happen. However, from deep in the human heart where priorities are set and choices are made, comes evil. Choices about the kind of food or the amount of food may be evil choices, but they are evil not in essence but in use. Neither does abstinence assure holiness, for that choice, too, may have evil motives.

Jesus lists human attitudes and actions by which a heart that is far from God expresses itself. Sin is not an outer affliction but an inner one.

Consider:

6. In what ways might something we take in—through the mouth, eyes or ears—feed the evil in the human heart? What clues does Jesus give in these verses about how to deal with the evil things that come from within us?

7. Reread Mark 7:15. In what ways have you allowed externals to separate you from God? When have you wrongfully imposed these spiritual "measuring rods" on others?

Mark 7:24-30

Tyre and Sidon were Gentile areas northwest of Galilee that were populated by Syrians and Phoenicians. Jesus was probably looking for some peace and quiet, but apparently Jesus' reputation had spread even to these areas. A Gentile woman came to him, fell at his feet and begged him to cure her daughter. Mark says the girl "had an unclean spirit," a condition that removed a person from fellowship with God. Thus the girl was doubly condemned: she was a pagan, outside of the covenant with God, a member of the "unchosen" people, *and* she was possessed.

The context of the chapter focuses the reader's attention on the word *unclean*. Earlier Jesus had repudiated the old beliefs that judged a person unclean for eating certain foods or for failing to observe traditions (7:1-23). He taught that only what issued out of the heart made a person morally impure.

In this story of the Syrophoenician woman, Jesus again abolishes religious standards for moral purity. Twentieth-century norms stumble over Jesus' reference to the woman as a dog. It is important to realize, however, that most rabbis would refuse to speak with any woman in public. Jesus' willingness to converse with a Gentile woman immediately communicated to her his true spirit, a spirit of gentleness and accessibility.

In response to Jesus' assertion that he came to give the good news to the Jewish people first (the children), the woman claims the scraps from God's table. Her rejoinder, full of humility and courage, reveals her as a woman of deep faith in a just and generous God. In rewarding her steadfast trust, Jesus declares her "clean," able to receive God's blessings, related to God in a way thought impossible by his Jewish opponents.

It is true, and justly so, that the children, the Jews, were fed first. As Paul wrote, "they are Israelites, and to them belong the adoption, the glory, the covenants, the giving of the law, the worship, and the promises; to them belong the patriarchs, and from them, according to the flesh, comes the Messiah" (Rom. 9:4-5). But Jesus shows that the "dogs," those rejected by human religious standards, may receive more, even

though they are second, when they are hungry and willingly admit it
(MT. 21:31-32).

Consider:

8. Who are the "children" today? Who are the "dogs"? What does Jesus' example indicate about contemporary religious prejudices?

9. The woman's reply impressed Jesus. Why? What did her response indicate to him? (Also read Mt. 15:21-28.)

Mark 7:31—8:26

This long section is best left undivided, for Mark brackets his account of the feeding of the four thousand with two parallel miracles of physical restoration. In both healings (7:31-37; 8:22-26), people come to Jesus and beg him to touch their disabled friend. In both instances, Jesus creates an atmosphere of privacy by moving away from the gaping crowd. Jesus' ministry in both cases includes Jesus' touch and spittle. Jesus commands both newly healed men to keep quiet about the events in order to avoid unwanted publicity.

The deaf man receives the gift of hearing by Jesus' command, "Eph-phatha!" Many believed that the spittle of a great man had curative powers. Jesus cooperates with this belief. His word, his touch and his saliva all become vehicles of his divine power. The man's inability to speak was clearly tied to his hearing impairment and when his ears are opened, "he spoke plainly."

The blind man receives the gift of sight by Jesus' two-touch restoration. This is a unique strategy in all the gospel accounts of Jesus' miracles. Clearly, Jesus has no pat formula for healing. Some are healed with one touch, some by two, some by a word from afar, some by spittle, some by mud, some by washing, some by brushing against the fringe hanging from Jesus' robe.

Mark's inclusion of a second account of miraculous feeding triggers questions about his intent in recounting this story. Some scholars point out the difference in the words used for *basket* in each story. In MARK 6:30-44, the word *basket* refers to a container commonly used by Jews. In 8:1-9, Mark uses a different word, one that refers to a much larger basket used by the Gentiles (ACTS 9:25). Commentators suggest that Mark thereby points out, symbolically, Jesus' intention and ability to satisfy the spiritual hungers of both Jews and Gentiles.

The piercing irony of the entire passage (7:31–8:26) comes in 8:11-12. Though the deaf receive hearing and the blind receive sight and the hungry are fed, the Pharisees demand "a sign from heaven," a demonstration of Jesus' credentials. Perhaps they want some divine signature blazoned across the sky. If so, Jesus flatly informs them that God has no intention of giving them such a sign.

Perhaps, though, the hearts of this group are so hard that they cannot receive the signs Jesus so generously gives. If this is the case, Jesus may be indicating that "he could do no deed of power" (6:5) for these people because of their unbelief.

In his private conversation with his disciples, Jesus warns them of this evil that corrupts by insisting that God meets human expectations. Jesus wishes to exceed human limitations, but the Pharisees and Herod prefer to play by their own rules. The disciples, however, have hardened hearts. Like the deaf man, they have ears but cannot hear; like the blind man, they have eyes that fail to see. They, too, need Jesus' healing touch and word of power.

Consider:

10. *What was the leaven of the Pharisees and of Herod (8:15)? From what Mark has told us so far (2:16, 24; 3:6; 6:14-29; 7:1-5), what do the Pharisees and Herod have in common? (Also read Lk. 23:8.) Where is this leaven present in your life? in the life of your community? in the Church?*

11. *Read Matthew 16:5-12. In what ways was the teaching of the Pharisees like leaven or yeast? What qualities of yeast make wrong teaching particularly dangerous?*

12. Compare the two healings in this section (7:31-37; 8:22-26). Which of Jesus' methods—immediate healing and victory over old ways or a gradual healing with stages of partial sight before full vision—most accurately reflects your spiritual journey? Why? If neither describes your experience, briefly summarize Jesus' personalized approach with you.

Group Activities

1. Discuss group members' responses to question 5 using the following steps:
   - Divide into pairs and invite each pair to brainstorm ideas about scriptural teachings that seem to conflict or even contradict each other.
   - Ask each pair to choose one area of tension and look up scripture passages that address that issue. Make sure that a Bible concordance is available.
   - Allow enough time for brief exploration before asking partners to present their issues and findings to the rest of the group.
   - After each issue has been presented, talk together about what the spirit of the law might be in each case.

2. By quoting Isaiah in Mark 7:6-7, Jesus charged the people with roleplaying honor for God instead of offering true worship. Many accuse Christians of hypocrisy and use that as a reason to avoid the Church.

   Divide into groups of three or four and ask each group to choose one contemporary Christian tradition that *can* invite hypocrisy. Invite groups to roleplay the tradition they chose. After groups have performed, discuss ways we can help our traditions enhance true worship rather than foster lip-service to God.

3. Reread MARK 7:33 and 8:23 and discuss the following:
   - Why does Jesus take these two individuals away from the crowds?
   - In what ways does coming away with Jesus facilitate the healing process?
   - How do contemporary Christians come away with Jesus?
   - What does a time alone with Jesus provide that time with him in larger groups, like church, cannot?

Explain to group members that Jesus wishes to "take them aside from the multitude privately" (7:33). Distribute index cards and crayons or felt markers. Ask group members to draw a simple picture that symbolizes for them Jesus' invitation (e.g., candle flame, open book, a pierced heart, etc.). Volunteers may wish to share their drawings. Group members may wish to keep these drawings as reminders of Jesus' touch.

Journal Meditation

Reread Jesus' list of evil things that come from within (7:20-23). On the left side of the space below, make a vertical list of the things that have come out of your heart that have made you feel "defiled" before God. Spend some time reflecting on each one and its frequency in your relationships with coworkers, family members, fellow believers.

Now, beside each thing listed, write a good action or attitude that can overcome that defiling thing. Spend some time reflecting on each of these and praying that God would replace the evil in your heart with these signs of true holiness.

Stepstone to Prayer

Lord, heal my heart of its uncleanness. Heal my...

Mark 8:27–9:32
The Leader's Identity

I N THIS SECTION, JESUS POSES THE CRUCIAL QUESTION of the gospel: "Who do you say that I am?" Every man, woman and child must at some time and in some way answer this question. To whom do you listen? Whom do you admire? Whom do you follow?

In these verses, Jesus reveals his true mission as the suffering servant and his true glory as the long-awaited Messiah. However, the disciples' messianic expectations miss the mark as they anticipate a Messiah who will rally the nation of Israel, conquer the world and forcefully impose God's rule on earth. Jesus redefines for them both his role and their relationship with him by explaining: he will rally all of God's people, not just Israel; he will conquer death before he conquers the world; and he will *become* humanity's righteousness rather than impose it. Read MARK 8:27–9:32.

Find The Facts

What title does Peter give Jesus? Who rebukes Jesus? Why does Jesus rebuke Peter? What will happen to the one who is ashamed of Jesus? Who accompanies Jesus up the mountain? What does God tell the disciples about Jesus? What could the disciples not do? Why?

Consider:

1. Underline every instance of the name Elijah. From these references, what can you tell of first-century beliefs about Elijah?

2. Circle every title given to Jesus. From these titles, what general conclusions can you draw about Jesus' identity and mission? Mark uses the title Son of man five times in this passage. From these instances, what do you think are the characteristics of the Son of man?

3. Which three verses in this section best define for you the way of the Lord? Why?

Mark 8:27—9:1

This section is the midpoint of Mark's gospel. From this point, everything rushes with increasing speed toward Jerusalem and the suffering of the cross. A new phase begins as the identity of Jesus, the leader of the new way, becomes clearer. Finally he steps out of the shadows by affirming his disciples' discovery of his true identity (Mt. 16:17).

Caesarea Philippi was a Gentile city where many cultural and spiritual streams converged. Earlier it had been a Canaanite center of worship for Baal, a fertility god. At one time it had been named after the Greek god of nature, Pan. It was also the place where a great marble temple had been built for the worship of Caesar, the godhead of the Roman pantheon. In this place of many philosophies and religions, Peter confesses that Jesus is the only "anointed one" (Heb., *Messiah*, Gk., *Christ*) of the only true God. Here, too, Jesus clearly teaches the disciples the meaning of his Messiahship.

The Jews had many opinions about the identity and role of the Messiah. Some expected him to be the greatest king of the earth, like a glorified David, who would raise an army and subdue all powers before him. Others were sure the Messiah would be a supernatural visitor from heaven who would accomplish the mighty reign of God with miraculous powers. Most people assumed that the rule of the Messiah would be a form of Jewish nationalism that subdued all the enemies of God, which included the Gentiles.

This must have been Peter's understanding when he confessed his faith in Jesus as the Messiah. For this reason, Jesus immediately begins to broaden the disciples' definition of the Messiah to include the suffering of the cross, an incomprehensible thought for the disciples. Peter takes Jesus aside to rebuke him for thinking that the death of a common criminal could be part of the messianic identity. Jesus knows that Peter's resistance comes as a temptation from Satan and human reason. Jesus faces the choice to go God's way, which includes suffering, death and resurrection, or the way of the wisdom of the world, a way of immediate gratification.

Not only will the Son of God most perfectly express the character of the Father by dying at the hands of those he loved, but he teaches that those who follow him and his way will also bear a cross. (The cross, an instrument of torture and disgrace, symbolized Rome's power over the world. It was reserved for criminals and political enemies who did not have Roman citizenship.) Those who follow Jesus will be on a collision course with the powers and authorities of this world. They will not escape the cross-like dilemmas of living and loving in this world while choosing entirely different values and beliefs.

Followers of Jesus must learn to say no to themselves and yes to him (8:34). Instincts, comforts, personal goals, success and security—all of which may be part of God's natural gifts—must take second place to following the way of Jesus, the Christ.

The Greek word for *life* in 8:35-37 is not *bios*, which refers to physical existence, but *psyche*, which refers to the soul, the activity of a person's spirit. By clinging to life as they had experienced it, as it had been defined for them by others, the disciples would lose their true selves. Old ways would inevitably become dead and unsatisfying. Life, Jesus says, is for wise spending in Christ's kingdom (8:35), not for safe hoarding or reckless wasting.

In 9:1, Jesus either speaks of the imminent transfiguration, which will reveal Jesus' true splendor, or he may refer to the glory of the rushing wind and tongues of fire at Pentecost (ACTS 2:1-4).

Consider:

4. What answers does twentieth-century society give to Jesus' question: "Who do people say that I am?"

5. Why must Jesus suffer, be rejected, killed and raised from the dead (8:31)? Why is this particular pathway necessary?

6. What is the difference between self-denial (8:34) and poor self-esteem or even self-hatred?

7. In what ways does society pressure us to "gain the whole world"? How do we end up forfeiting our lives?

Mark 9:2-13

In every account (9:2-10; Mт. 17:1-13; Lk. 9:28-36, 44-45), Jesus' transfiguration immediately follows Peter's confession and the disciples' first lesson about Jesus' course of shame, suffering and final vindication. In Christ's way, belief lays the foundation for sight. The transfiguration could no more have preceded the confession of faith than could Jesus' resurrection have preceded his crucifixion.

Three of the disciples see the truth about Jesus (Rev. 1:12-16). His outer appearance is transformed so that the glory of his inner divine life can be revealed. The sudden appearance of two other witnesses also testifies to the magnificence of the occasion.

Moses represents the written law of God, which sustained the covenant. Elijah, the greatest of the prophets in Israel's history, represents the spoken word of God, which sustained the promises of a new relationship with God. All that the law desired to accomplish, but could not, and all that the prophets longed to see come to pass, but did not, this Jesus brought to fulfillment.

Peter wants to freeze the moment and build a shrine, but he babbles out of wonder and fear. His proposal puts Jesus on a par with the two greatest figures in Jewish history, but God exalts Jesus only and redirects the disciples' attention, devotion and fullest obedience to this One who fully bears the love of the Father.

Jesus alone accompanies his friends down the mountain and into the valley. Again, the disciples cannot understand where suffering fits into the mission of the Son of God. Seeing Elijah triggers their messianic expectations, which included the powerful ministry of Elijah who would "restore all things." Jesus says that, in John the Baptist, Elijah has already come; and if he suffered so, how much more will the Anointed One undergo?

8. In what ways is Jesus the fulfillment of the law and the prophets? (Read Mt. 5: 17-18.)

9. What did Jesus' transfiguration reveal about him? What does it communicate to twentieth-century Christians? What new truth does it reveal to you about Jesus?

10. Compare 9:7 with 1:11. What significance do you see in this double affirmation of Jesus' relationship with God?

11. In what sense did John the Baptist "restore all things"? Who comes now in a ministry of restoration and preparation for Jesus' second coming?

Mark 9:14-32

While three of the disciples witness Jesus' transfiguration, the others struggle to carry on the ministry. Their efforts, however, dissolve into arguments. The desperate father and son stand by helplessly while the disciples, unable to drive out the unclean spirit, defend their work against the criticisms of the scribes. Mark presents a stark contrast between Jesus' word of power and the disciples' many words of futility. Though Jesus had given them authority over evil spirits (6:7), he clearly expected them to exercise it with and through prayer—not a quick little request thrown to God in an emergency, but an uninterrupted intimacy with God. The disciples' failure to pray showed a lack of understanding about their utter dependence on God.

Jesus rebukes the unbelief of the whole crowd, for such unbelief prevents miracles (6:5-6). His rhetorical questions in 9:19 point out that his followers must quickly learn his ways, for they will soon be called to carry on his work without his visible presence.

The spirit's possession afflicted the boy with epileptic-like seizures and the inability to speak, with the added purpose of destroying the boy (9:22). The anxious father, having lost hope by the disciples' bungling, wonders if their Master can do any better. Jesus' response redirects the issue back to the father. Neither God's ability nor Jesus' willingness were in question, only the man's faith. Jesus' great claim, "All things can be done for the one who believes," however, is not a spiritual credit card that can be used to satisfy egocentric desires. God had revealed Jesus as the model for the highest moral and ethical demands and as the one who could make possible the deepest fellowship with God. Within the parameters of Jesus' way, all the possibilities and purposes of God's kingdom are available for the taking.

12. What principles of faith can you find in this passage? In what ways is the disciples' need for faith similar to or different from the father's need for faith? With which character do you relate the most? Why?

13. Do you think Jesus' statement in 9:23 has any qualifications, limitations or other restrictions? If so, what are they? If not, why do so few Christians experience this power? What does prayer do? How does it work?

14. What new aspect of the passion does Jesus reveal in 9:31? (Compare with 8:31.) Why do you think Mark includes that here? What does it indicate about the relationship between the disciples and Jesus?

15. *What impressions of Jesus does our ministry give the people around us? In what ways do we get caught in futile arguments while needy people stand by waiting for our touch? In what ways does our ministry reflect negatively on Jesus? reflect positively on Jesus?*

Group Activities

1. Dramatize the transfiguration and the story of the boy's healing. Begin by listing on chalkboard, whiteboard or newsprint all the characters or types of groups represented. Then divide group members so that all the main characters are assigned. Ask a volunteer to narrate the story while the characters speak their parts, reading from the scripture with emotion and actions. When finished, discuss:

   • How did you feel as the character?

   • What new insights do you have into that person's feelings?

   • How does the whole group feel about the main people in the story? Why?

2. On chalkboard, whiteboard or newsprint, make two columns and label them *Moses* and *Jesus*. Then read Exodus 24:15-18 and 33:12-23 and compare these accounts with the story of the transfiguration (9:2-9). What are the similarities? the differences? List responses in the appropriate columns. Discuss:

   • Why do you think both events took place on a mountain?

   • What does the cloud symbolize?

   • In what ways does Jesus' experience transcend and fulfill Moses' experience?

3. Ask group members to call out the characteristics of the boy's seizures. List these on chalkboard, whiteboard or newsprint. Then divide into pairs and ask partners to think of ways that spiritual enemies afflict your community with similar characteristics, either physically or spiritually.

   Reassemble the group and invite pairs to share the examples they found. Spend some time praying for the Lord to heal you and your community. Close by reading aloud PSALM 6:8-10:

   > Depart from me, all you workers of evil,
   >   for the Lord has heard the sound of my weeping.
   > The Lord has heard my supplication;
   >   the Lord accepts my prayer.
   > All my enemies shall be ashamed and struck with terror;
   >   they shall turn back, and in a moment be put to shame.

Journal Meditation

Reread MARK 9:14-27 slowly and prayerfully. Then choose one of the following exercises:

• Close your eyes and imagine that you are the boy. You feel a seizure coming on you. You are in great danger of being cast into the nearby fire and water. Your father is near. He grabs and holds you to keep you from danger. Now he lifts you and carries you to Jesus and sets you down at his feet. Imagine what Jesus does and how you feel. Describe your feelings. Write a prayer that asks God to free you from your most controlling sin and weakness.

• Close your eyes and imagine that you are the father. You have constantly watched over your son, always hesitant to leave him, fearing that the unclean spirit will overtake him while you are gone. You brought your son, but Jesus is gone and his disciples have been unable to help. Suddenly Jesus arrives and challenges your hopelessness. Describe your feelings. Now make a list of the situations in which you are as despairing and divided as the boy's father when he said, "I believe; help my unbelief!" Listen for Jesus' response.

Stepstone to Prayer

Come, Lord Jesus, and deliver us from evil...

Mark 9:33–10:52
On the Way with the Lord

JESUS RETURNS TO CAPERNAUM ONE MORE TIME before he begins his final journey to Jerusalem. In these last days before his triumphal entry into Jerusalem, Jesus' teaching focuses on the spirit his followers must have to accompany him all the way to the cross. In the events of the previous chapters, Jesus' disciples discovered his true identity as the Messiah (8:29; 9:2-3). In the events of these verses, Jesus describes the new identity of those who can receive the kingdom of God.

Here we may find the most accurate depictions of the human hunger for power. Jesus counters these occasions of pride with a new definition of power: followers of Jesus will discover true power as they humbly serve those they may deem beneath them. Those who lust for power as the world defines it—by wealth, status or privilege—will find it extremely difficult to enter God's kingdom. Read MARK 9:33–10:52.

Find The Facts

List the people Jesus encounters on his journey to Jerusalem. What events in these verses include children? What did Moses teach about divorce? What does Jesus teach about divorce? What does Jesus invite the rich man to do in order to inherit eternal life? What new information does Jesus give about his imminent death (8:31; 9:31; 10:33-34)? What favor did James and John ask of Jesus? What title did blind Bartimaeus give to Jesus?

Mark 9:33-41

The disciples are caught in a typical squabble about greatness and rank. According to Jesus, humility and service are the characteristic marks of success in the kingdom of God (9:35). In contrast, the disciples quarrel about qualifications for the administration of an earthly messianic kingdom. They assume their close relationship with the Messiah will result in privileged positions of power in the new order.

This vision of success obstructs the way of the Lord, a way of humble openness to those the world may overlook. Jesus says that, as they honor a child, true disciples honor Christ. The child symbolizes all who are needy, helpless and vulnerable, all those who cannot return a favor or profit us in any way. Jesus takes the child into his nurturing embrace, demonstrating the manner in which we must receive the weak.

The disciples clearly do not grasp the essence of Jesus' teaching. In verse 38, the disciples show that they are still caught up in their struggle with prestige and control. They rebuke the man using Jesus' name to cast out demons because he was not one of the inner group. The disciples assume that Jesus will approve of their disciplinary action.

The man casting out demons in Jesus' name was one of these little children who needed to be received and encouraged, not discouraged or made to feel inadequate and unacceptable. The man understands Jesus' authority and concern for other hurt persons, and thus proves that he is in the kingdom, though unconnected with its "official" form of discipleship. The disciples' narrow vision of the kingdom compels them to exclude the man; Jesus commends him and includes him.

A huge set of global and ecumenical questions opens up here. "Whoever is not against us is for us" (9:40). In what ways, outside our limited vision of the Christian faith, is the will of God being done? What attitudes does Jesus call us to have in regard to those who are not a part of our small corner of the kingdom? Perhaps he invites us to a spirit of tolerance and a willingness to suspend quick judgments.

Jesus' disciples must learn to rejoice when Christlike truth is taught or when a person is lifted up and made whole, even when the benefactor is not "one of us." Even the smallest action done in Jesus' name, like quenching the thirst of a dry throat or soul, merits a great reward in God's kingdom.

3. How does Jesus feel about ambition? Contrast Jesus' definition of success with the disciples' ideas about it.

4. What kind of attitude is needed to receive a child? Who are the "children" in today's society? In what ways is your Christian community receiving these individuals? In what ways do you receive them?

5. Compare Jesus' view of the kingdom of God with your own. Whom have you unconsciously wished to exclude from the kingdom? In what ways do these verses enable you to broaden your understanding of the kingdom?

Mark 9:42-50

The phrase "little ones" connects this passage with the two preceding it. Jesus has shown the disciples that those they consider of little importance—the weak, the unqualified, the outsider—have great value in God's eyes. Here he stresses this again by warning his disciples of the dire consequences of causing another, no matter how "insignificant," to sin.

Sinful behavior has serious results. Influencing others to their harm will ultimately come back to harm us. Sin is a dark investment against ourselves, but to teach others to sin is far worse for it opens the door to hell. How much more graphic could Jesus have been when he said that to cause anyone to stumble on God's pathway is more deadly than to be thrown into deep water with an anchor around our necks? Both indirect instruction, like poor modeling, or direct instruction, like false teaching, proves fatal.

Jesus tells his disciples that it is better to be maimed than to let sinful behavior draw them into hell. In the same way that a physician will amputate a part of the body to save the patient's life, so the true disciple will cut off any area of his or her life that becomes a source of sin, no matter how painful the sacrifice. The examples Jesus uses—the hand, the foot and the eye—represent otherwise good and healthy parts of life. Jesus tells his disciples that severing themselves from sin is not radical enough; they must sever themselves also from the source of sin. He insists that entering "life," the kingdom of God, is worth any loss.

Hell (Gk., *Gehenna*) refers to the valley of Hinnom, a gully just southwest of Jerusalem. This ravine was originally the place where the Canaanites offered human sacrifices to Molech (2 Chr. 28:3). Later it became the city's garbage dump. Its stench and the smoldering smoke it sent up was an apt symbol for life apart from the love of God.

The word *fire* in verse 49 makes the transition from the punishment warned of in verse 48 to the counsel in verse 50. Fire both consumes the unrighteous and purifies the righteous. Only a consuming passion for God's will can make possible the sacrifice and discipline required to enter God's kingdom.

In first-century Israel, salt was invaluable as a preservative, as a healing agent and as a seasoning. Its peculiar properties qualified it as a precious commodity, but when it lost its characteristics, either by diluting it or contaminating it with an excessive amount of another substance, it retained no value whatsoever.

Consider:

6. *What are some positive or neutral areas of contemporary life that may cause sin? What kind of sacrifice would it take to eliminate these areas from your life? Which of these do you find the most painful to contemplate sacrificing? Why?*

7. *Suggest a spiritual equivalent for each of the qualities of salt. How salty is your faith community? Where has your spiritual life lost its saltiness?*

8. In what ways do the qualities of salt enable Christian brothers and sisters to "be at peace with one other"?

Mark 10:1-12

A most serious issue of Jesus' time was divorce. The scripture gives high honor to the sanctity of marriage. Yet the common Jewish practice in Jesus' time was calloused. A statement of release, written by a rabbi, could be easily attained at the man's request. Jewish law treated the wife as a possession without any personal legal rights, a person at the complete disposal of the husband (DT. 24:1). She could be cast aside for the most trivial of reasons.

The Pharisees do not seek wisdom, but wish to "test" Jesus and perhaps trick him into saying something that will make him lose credibility in the peoples' eyes. The Pharisees pit Jesus against Moses.

Jesus reveals the original reason for Moses' permissive stance and most cleverly counters it with an even older and higher authority—the original plan of God in creation (GEN. 1:27; 2:23-24). Jesus restores the God-given gift of marriage to its high place in God's good order and calls his disciples to follow this principle in their marital relationships.

Moses' "compromise" was intended to regulate the consequences of divorce, not to free the husband to do as he pleased. Jesus teaches that marriage is meant to have a permanency that cannot be set aside by a piece of paper. The Pharisees seem more concerned with personal freedom and legal nitpicking; Jesus redirects their attention to the centrality of the stable home, the dignity of the wife and the spiritual depth of the marriage bond. Jesus' more confidential words to his disciples (10:10-12) put the husband and wife on an equal level, an unheard-of premise in first-century Israel.

Consider:

9. Read Genesis 2:22-24. What kind of relationship do these verses describe? Do you think this description is relevant or applicable to contemporary marriages? Why or why not?

10. Compare what seemed to be happening in marriages in Jesus' time and what you see happening in the twentieth-century. What are the similarities and the differences? What do you think Jesus would say to his followers today?

Mark 10:13-31

In these verses Jesus describes those who are able to receive the kingdom of God. His example again elevates the spirit of a child, though different qualities are here emphasized. In 9:36-37, Jesus calls for a spirit of humility that can receive someone as insignificant as a child. Here Jesus speaks of receiving the kingdom of God with an open and willing spirit, like the eagerness and trustfulness of a child.

Many find that it is often more pleasurable to give something to a child than to an adult. A child can receive a gift without any trace of self-consciousness, without awkwardness, without getting caught in a tangle of embarrassed gratitude. The kingdom of God, Jesus says, must be received as a gift freely given. It is not a reward to political favorites nor is it granted only to those who score points with God through any virtue.

The rich man described in 10:17-22 believes the kingdom—eternal life—belongs to those who merit it. He had kept all the "do nots" of God's law. Jesus loves the man for his zeal, his eagerness, indeed, his childlike longing to please God. The man's ambition was good and right. His failure, however, lies in his desire to rely on his accomplishments. He did not wish to receive eternal life, but to earn it. Jesus wants the man to follow him, but clearly sees that such a course would be impossible unless the man could first discard the burden of his own success.

Jesus turns to his disciples and revolutionizes their understanding about wealth. The Jews believed that anyone who had an abundance of God's blessings must be a good person whom God wished to reward. Much of the Old Testament teaches the general principle that God rewards the righteous and brings grief to the wicked. In fact, a wealthy man might be even better situated spiritually by his ability to devote more time to worship and more money to charity. No wonder that the disciples are astonished to hear that riches may actually impede spiritual progress.

Yet Jesus' words in 10:27 redirect the disciples' attention to the divine grace that can enable anyone to enter God's kingdom. He echoes the lesson about receiving the kingdom as a child: salvation is a gift; whether rich or poor, it is humanly impossible to earn salvation.

Watching the young man leave, Peter said, "Look, we have left everything and followed you..." (10:28). So what will be our reward? is his unspoken question. Here Jesus hints at the wonderful intimacy of the Church, a community a hundred times greater than anything sacrificed for the sake of God's work. He adds, though, that it will come "with persecutions." This world will not understand and will violently reject the way of Christ, but this will not affect the unfolding relationships that a common faith will generate.

Consider:

11. *List the childlike characteristics that enable a person to receive the kingdom of God. Make another list of those characteristics that prevent a person from receiving God's kingdom. Which list best describes you?*

12. *What is it about riches (or any possession, passion or personal accomplishment) that can prevent someone from receiving the kingdom of God? In what way do your "riches" keep you from following Christ?*

13. How well do you think the Church lives up to Jesus' description of a community rich in property and relationships?

Mark 10:32-52

Jesus resolutely walks on down the Jordan valley toward the oasis town of Jericho. Those who accompany him wonder at his courage and perhaps question his wisdom in nearing a city that harbors those who condemn him. For the third time, Jesus senses the need to warn his disciples of what will happen in Jerusalem.

Jesus has repeatedly spoken to his disciples of the kingdom's demand for humility. His decision to give himself over to mockery, torture and finally a humiliating death for his enemies exemplifies his many words about serving the lowly. But the disciples are spiritually blind. As Jesus steels himself on the journey for his ultimate test of obedience, two of his most trusted disciples come to him and attempt to gain an advantage over the rest of the disciples (10:35-40).

James and John are driven more by the goal of recognition as Jesus' chief administrators than by the way of the Lord. When Jesus speaks of his violent end, they can only think of personal gain. Jesus understands that their request is one of ignorance. They still have no idea of the demands that will be placed on those who wish to walk in the way of the Lord. To "drink the cup" was a common idiom meaning to participate fully in someone else's experiences. Jesus refers to his suffering as a baptism, or immersion.

It is no surprise that this attempt to gain power over the other disciples caused bitterness and anger. Again Jesus seizes the moment to teach about true greatness. God-blessed ambition does not seek to gain power over others but focuses instead on serving others in ways that accomplish the will of God for them and in them.

Jesus sees that the whole world is trapped in a power-hungry system that exalts one ego over another. Jesus says that his whole purpose in coming was to ransom, or purchase the release of, those enslaved by this system. Only the sacrifice of Jesus' life can pay the price of human freedom. Yet this new freedom does not make men and women independent of one another, but liberates them to imitate Jesus' example of service.

The healing of Bartimaeus concludes Mark's account of Jesus' public ministry outside of Jerusalem. Jesus' days are numbered. Jesus passes through Jericho, a city approximately 15 miles from Jerusalem, undoubtedly accompanied by many other pilgrims on their way to the holy city for Passover. Many beggars commonly lined these routes, particularly during the days before and after Jewish festivals.

Jesus' question, "What is it you want me to do for you?" (10:36, 51), ties together the disciples' lesson about servanthood and Bartimaeus's healing. Clearly Bartimaeus has heard of Jesus of Nazareth, his compassion and his miraculous power. Bartimaeus refuses to be discouraged by his lowly position, his inability to find Jesus easily, or by the rebukes of the crowd.

Bartimaeus calls Jesus "Son of David," an unmistakable messianic title (2 Sam. 7:4-5, 11-16; Is. 11:1), and seems confident that Jesus will in fact have mercy on him. Bartimaeus seems able to see Jesus more clearly than do the disciples (Jn. 9:1-41).

14. In your own words, answer the disciples' argument in 9:34. Who do you know who is truly great? In what ways has that person been a "slave of all"?

15. Where do you see evidence of the kind of authority that Jesus describes in 10:42? In what ways do Christians also fall into the trap of status and authority? How well do you think the Church demonstrates mutual servanthood?

16. Compare James and John's request of Jesus with that of Bartimaeus. How would you describe the two disciples' spirit? Bartimaeus's spirit? In what ways are you blind to Jesus?

Group Activities

1. Invite group members to share their answers to question 11. Record their responses on chalkboard, whiteboard or newsprint. Discuss
   - Is our community receiving the kingdom like a child? Why or why not?

   Briefly evaluate every major church event (worship services, board meetings, social times, small groups, etc.) to see if the childlike characteristics are present or missing. Brainstorm together about ways in which methods or attitudes need to change.

2. List together on chalkboard, whiteboard or newsprint those persons whom contemporary society considers to be "children" (i.e., people who do not seem to benefit us in any way). These may include children, disabled people, poorly educated individuals, the poor, minorities, women, etc. Now discuss ways that your church receives and honors these individuals in your worship services, in your committees, in your homes, etc.

3. Invite group members to call out different forms of "wealth" that can impede a person from entering the kingdom of God. Now divide into groups of two or three and discuss:
   - Why was the rich man unable to part with his possessions?
   - What keeps us from letting go of our "possessions"?
   - How can we help one another to enter the kingdom of God?

4. A form of Bartimaeus's initial cry to Jesus has become known as the Jesus Prayer: *Jesus, have mercy on me, a sinner.* On chalkboard, whiteboard or newsprint list the different elements of Bartimaeus's cry. Discuss:
   - What makes his cry an excellent model for prayer?

   Close your time together with a few minutes of prayer. Invite each group member to pray aloud, beginning his or her prayer with Bartimaeus's cry.

Journal Meditation

Close your eyes and imagine Jesus coming to you. He asks, "What is it you want me to do for you?" What is your most burning request? Record this below.

Now reflect for a few moments on what your request of Jesus reveals. What does your request reveal about your spirit? What does your request reveal about your faith in Jesus? What does your request reveal about your deepest desires? If your request were granted, would it enable you to "follow Jesus on the way" (10:52)? Why or why not?

Stepstone to Prayer

Lord, in order to follow you more closely, I need...

Mark 11–12
Opposition to the Way of the Lord

THE LAST ACT OF THE DIVINE DRAMA BEGINS with a declaration of kingship. Jesus enters Jerusalem, beginning his last week with the shouts of Hosanna! ringing in his ears. Jesus will fill these last days with numerous demonstrations of his authority over God's people, his complete control over his own fate, and his gentle willingness to submit to the violent plans of his enemies. The political machinery that has opposed him at every step now gears up to grind him into the grave.

Before the bloody execution, those in religious authority seek publicly acceptable reasons to doom him. Again and again, they come to Jesus armed with plots designed to entangle Jesus in verbal traps about difficult social problems that will cause him either to lose the people's favor or to incur the Roman wrath.

Jesus clearly discerns their hypocrisy, wisely avoids their traps, and demonstrates to all that his death will be due to the will of God, not to the cunning of his enemies.

Jesus' last days are full of "living parables," actions performed in order to teach a truth. His final teachings call his followers to holy lives of prayer, of civil responsibility, of undiluted devotion to God, of love for others and of simple generosity. Read MARK 11–12.

Find the Facts

What do the people do as Jesus enters Jerusalem? What does Jesus do when he enters the temple area? What reaction does this bring from those in authority? Why do the chief priests and the scribes want to destroy Jesus? How do the Pharisees and Herodians try to trap Jesus? What riddle do the Sadducees pose to Jesus? What is the greatest commandment?

Consider:

1. *What does Jesus communicate about his kingship in these chapters? What do the events of these chapters indicate about the kind of king the people expect Jesus to be? When have you experienced a great difference between what you expect of Jesus and what Jesus actually wants for your life?*

2. *Underline each of the questions asked of Jesus in these two chapters. What deeper issue does each question address? Suggest a contemporary equivalent for each of these questions.*

3. *Make a notation in the margins of your text each time Jesus quotes from the Old Testament. What does this indicate to you about Jesus? In what ways does his knowledge of scripture empower him? What application do you find to your own life?*

Mark 11:1-11

As Jesus approaches the holy city, he first passes through two suburbs of Jerusalem, Bethphage and Bethany, where by prearrangement a young donkey was ready for his use. It had never been ridden before, probably because Jesus wants it to symbolize the temple offerings, which had never been used for any purpose (NUM. 19:2; DT. 21:3; 1 SAM. 6:7). In the first century, a king who entered a city on a mission of peace would ride a donkey; a king who came as a conqueror would ride a horse.

Jesus' action here may be called a "living parable" or prophetic symbolism. Old Testament prophets would often communicate God's message by enacting a drama designed to symbolize the truth that the people needed to hear. For example, the prophet Jeremiah was instructed to purchase a clay jar, gather the leaders of the people and break the jar in their presence. This visually reinforced his message about God's plan to shatter Jerusalem (JER. 19:1-13).

Obviously Jesus does not set up the triumphal entry in order to gain the misunderstood praise of the people. Jesus was not a glory-seeker. He arranges his entry into Jerusalem in order to communicate a message about his role as Messiah and King. By riding on a donkey, Jesus clearly tells the people that he comes as their Messiah, for this action was prophesied about the Messiah in ZECHARIAH 9:9:

> Rejoice greatly, O daughter of Zion!
>   Shout aloud, O daughter of Jerusalem!
> Lo, your king comes to you;
>   triumphant and victorious is he,
> humble and riding on a donkey,
>   on a colt, the foal of a donkey.

By publicly claiming to be the Messiah, Jesus demands a choice from the people. Either they accept him or they reject him. Neutrality is no longer an option.

The people shout "Hosanna!", a cry of supplication (lit., "save now") and praise. The words come from PSALM 118, a hymn celebrating a military victory. Though their words are appropriate, the people use them to indicate their hope that Jesus will conquer their enemies through might. This popular view of the Messiah was wrong, and Jesus' entry was designed to correct their vision. God conquers, yes, but by loving sacrifice, not by bloodshed and subjugation.

Consider:

4. *Read Psalm 118. What clues does this psalm give you about what is in the minds of the people as Jesus enters? What nationalistic fears and hopes are evident in this passage? Where are these feelings present today in the Church?*

5. *What feelings do you think this event triggers in the Jewish leaders? Why? When have you felt the need to defend the status quo? In what other ways has Jesus "threatened" your sense of security?*

Mark 11:12-33

This section tells of another "living parable," Jesus' cursing of the fruitless fig tree. During Jesus' last week, he stays in Bethany. On his way into the city on the morning after his spectacular entry, he curses a fig tree that has no figs on it. Jesus' behavior is unreasonable since it was not yet time for the tree to bear fruit. Only later, on their way back to the city the next morning, do the disciples hear Jesus' message symbolized by the withered fig tree.

Though Jesus entered the city in peace, he now changes his tactics. His violent behavior in the temple area demonstrates his authority and forces the Jewish leaders to deal with his claims. The top of Mount Zion was set aside as the holy place. Deep inside the walled courts, porticos and buildings was a small room called the most holy place. This was where the ark of the covenant sat, the dwelling place of the glory of God (1 KG. 8:10). The high priest entered this room only once a year to make atonement for the people.

An outer room with lamps and incense burners was tended by small groups of priests on a rotating basis. This area stood in the court of the priests where sacrifices were offered. Beyond this was the court of the

Israelites where Jewish men gathered and where animals were brought to the priests. The court of women, used for prayer, was beyond this. The outermost area was the court of the Gentiles, a quiet place where foreigners could come, inquire of rabbis about faith in Yahweh, pray and personally seek the Lord. It was Israel's architectural answer to its call to be a light and a blessing to the nations (Is. 56:7).

It was this outer court, reserved for Gentile inquiry, that had been turned into a marketplace and a shortcut across town. The families of the chief priests had control of the area and its business. Animals intended for sacrifices were sure to cost more here, but, if they were not bought here, they would be declared blemished and unusable.

Since an animal had to be purchased with temple currency, money changers were required to make the exchange of all foreign currency. This was done at a significant profit, which was shared with the priests. Jesus is angry, both because of the unjust way the Jewish pilgrims were being treated and because the mission of Israel to the whole world was being so grossly ignored (JER. 7-11).

The day after Jesus' upset of the temple practices, the disciples notice that the fig tree has completely withered. Jesus uses the visual focus to speak to his disciples about fruitlessness and fruitfulness. By cleansing the temple, Jesus had dramatically exposed Israel's fruitlessness. Such fruitlessness, Jesus says, will be judged.

On the other hand, a true relationship with God, as demonstrated by faithful prayer and generous forgiveness, will result in fruit beyond human expectation. Indeed, Jesus had expected the impossible of the fig tree since it was not yet in season. Yet through the disciples' faith in God, the impossible will become possible.

In verses 27-33, the religious leaders show that they understand Jesus' message. He had officially judged the temple authorities, and they demand to know the source of his authority. Jesus' question, while managing to avoid a direct conflict that could provoke an arrest before he is ready, also manages to communicate clearly that Jesus' authority comes from God, as John the Baptist has indicated (1:7-8; JN. 1:29-34).

6. What does Jesus' violent action in the temple indicate to you about his values? his methods? When have you or someone you know been righteously angry at some injustice? Why do we often fail to act as boldly in such circumstances?

7. The chief priest and scribes fear Jesus. What are they afraid of? To what degree do you think fear prevents people today from accepting Jesus? What are people afraid of today?

8. In your imagination, transfer Jesus' actions in the temple to the Church. What would he drive out? What would he overturn? What would he prevent? Consider his cleansing in your life. What areas meant for worship, prayer, study and sharing need to be cleansed?

9. What principles of prayer can you glean from Mark 12:22-25? In what ways does faithful prayer enable you to bear fruit? How does Jesus' further teaching in John 15:1-16 help you to understand this passage?

Mark 12:1-12

When the religious leaders refused to answer Jesus' question in 11:30, they showed that they were more interested in maintaining their positions and privileges than in identifying the truth. They therefore became ineffective as priests and hindrances to God's work, as do all who seek to please themselves rather than serve the truth. Jesus' parable of the vineyard demonstrates this.

This parable is based on the social structure of Jesus' time. Wealthy landlords who owned great parcels of land would rent the land out to tenants. The landlords would rarely make an appearance, only requiring a share of the produce as the rent payment. If a landlord died without an heir, the land could be claimed by the tenants.

In this parable, the tenants prove untrustworthy and treacherous. The story inevitably reminds Jesus' audience of the prophet Isaiah's song of the vineyard (Is. 5:1-7), in which God judges Israel for its failure to produce righteousness and justice. In that song, Israel hears of God's sorrowful decision to punish the nation.

In Jesus' story, the tenants assume the landlord is dead and the son is coming to claim his inheritance. They assassinate the son and believe that their claim to the vineyard can now no longer be disputed. Jesus quotes another verse from PSALM 118 to show that, though they easily rid themselves of the son as the final obstacle to their desires, that son will become the key to God's kingdom.

As Jesus tells his story, he makes clear that the leaders' refusal to accept God's prophets, and, ultimately, God's Son, will compel God to offer the kingdom to others who will prove more faithful.

Consider:

10. What does the parable reveal to you about God?

11. Why do you think Psalm 118:22-23 became a key verse to early Christians (Acts 4:11; Eph. 2:20; 1 Pet. 2:7)? What does it indicate to you about Jesus? about the kingdom of God?

12. In what ways might this parable call the Church to repent? In what ways has the Church refused to give God the fruit of the vineyard?

Mark 12:13-27

The leaders of the temple now get serious about finding cause to arrest Jesus. They send their debaters from the Pharisees, the Herodians and the Sadducees to trap him into saying something self-incriminating.

The Pharisees and Herodians were not natural collaborators. The latter supported the rule of Herod, which derived its authority from Rome. The Pharisees preferred Jewish independence and resented much of Rome's intrusions into their religious life. These parties join forces in their attempt to destroy Jesus. In these verses, they place before him the burning issue of paying taxes to Rome, an obligation that every loyal Jew deeply resented.

Jesus' correct and balanced response amazes them. The image of Caesar on the coin reminds them that the image of God was "stamped" into the soul of every human being (Gen. 1:26-27). Jesus makes it clear that civil authority has its proper place in God's scheme, and the government needs to be supported within the limits of a commitment to follow Christ (Rom. 13:1-7).

Jesus' conclusion in 12:17 reinforces the point of his parable in 12:1-12: The leaders were more concerned about their own rights, political and religious, and failed to give to God what belonged to God.

The Sadducees were a smaller religious party composed mainly of upper-class Jews who controlled the priestly roles of the temple. They cooperated with Roman rule in order to preserve their own positions. They officially recognized only the first five books of scripture, the Pentateuch, and denied many of the beliefs that other parts of the scripture taught. One of the tenets they rejected was the resurrection of the dead, a teaching that they felt could not be demonstrated from the Pentateuch.

Thus they come to Jesus with a tricky argument about a woman who was married to seven brothers. This was theoretically possible under the social responsibility of a Jewish male to raise up sons for a deceased brother who had had no children (Dt. 25:5-6). The law was originally given to protect a childless widow and to guarantee the just inheritance of family property.

The Sadducees' example reflects the attitude that the woman is the property of her husband. They try to point out how ridiculous it is to believe in a resurrection where her duty to her husband, all seven of them, would continue beyond the grave.

Jesus does not hesitate to point out the error of their teaching, basing his answer on the part of the scripture that the Sadducees accept. They fail to understand the power of God, which can raise the dead into a life that is far more than a mere improvement on this one. The resurrection is beyond present human experience.

Consider:

13. What does this passage say about governmental authority and liberty of conscience? What spheres of contemporary life belong to Caesar and what spheres of life belong to God? When might the claims of the government conflict with your loyalty to God?

14. Read 1 Corinthians 15:35-54. In your own words, what are Paul and Jesus saying about the resurrection? Does the hope of a new life motivate you in this life? Why or why not?

Mark 12:28-44

The attempt to condense the entire law into one great commandment was not an uncommon exercise for many teachers of the law. In contrast to the mocking and hypocritical attitude of the Pharisees, Herodians and Sadducees, one scribe comes to Jesus with a sincere desire to discover truth.

Jesus answers by combining the Shema, the central creed of Jewish monotheism (DT. 6:4), with a commandment from Leviticus that calls for love of neighbor (LEV. 19:18). Every devout Jew knew and used the Shema, which began worship in the synagogue and was written and rolled up in small leather boxes, worn on foreheads and wrists (EX. 13:1-10; MT. 23:5).

Jesus' unique combination of love for God and neighbor shows that the two naturally reflect one another. Love for God is primary, but it will always result in a love for others. The scribe's response to Jesus' teaching shows an intense love for God and a wise understanding of God's priorities (Hos. 6:6).

Jesus turns the tables in the next few verses. He too offers a trick question, though his is not designed to manipulate his audience. The scriptural riddle Jesus poses deals with David's prophetic words about the Messiah (Ps. 110:1). Jesus shows that the Messiah, the Son of David, will be more than a mere descendant of an earthly king, for he will be David's Lord.

Once again Jesus tries to turn the people's hopes away from a warrior-like Messiah. *Lord* was the title that was normally used in place of God's personal name when referring to God. The earthly king they looked for was really going to be a revelation of God. Jesus stresses the relationship with God, not the political and military power of the Messiah.

Jesus then contrasts the empty greatness of the religious leaders (12:38-40) with the true greatness of the poor widow who gave to God what belonged to God. This woman draws no attention to herself, sacrificing all that she has out of honor for God. Undoubtedly her small contribution could not accomplish much for God's work, but Jesus says that gifts are not measured by the results they achieve but by the motivation of the giver. This woman, rather than the scribes, is the model for worshiping God.

Consider:

15. What are some ways that you can love God with all your heart? with all your understanding? with all your strength?

16. Define love for your neighbor. With twentieth-century technology, we come into contact with masses of people daily from around the world. Who is your neighbor today? Can we realistically love them all? Why or why not?

17. What is the relationship between our love for our neighbor and our love for God?

18. *Make a list of the qualities demonstrated by the poor widow. What do you think she values most in life? How can you become more like her?*

Group Activities

Copy as many of the following assignments onto index cards as you need for small groups of two or three:

Group #1: MARK 11:12-14, 20-25
- On a sheet of newsprint, draw a fig tree.
- Reread your passage and brainstorm what "fruit" might please Jesus.
- Using the Bible concordance, look up other scriptures that refer to the fruit God expects from our lives.
- Cut out construction-paper figs and label each one with a fruit you have discovered in scripture; tape these to your fig tree.

Group #2: MARK 12:13-17
- On a sheet of newsprint, draw a moneybag.
- Reread your passage and brainstorm what "coins" we owe to God.
- Using the Bible concordance, look up other scriptures that refer to things we have that belong to God.
- Cut out construction-paper coins and label each one with something owed to God; tape these to your money bag.

Group #3: Mark 12:28-34

- On a sheet of newsprint, draw two stone tablets.
- Reread your passage and brainstorm ways in which we can love the Lord our God and ways in which we can love our neighbor.
- Using the Bible concordance, look up other scriptures that refer to love for God or neighbor.
- On one tablet, record what you have discovered about loving God. On the other tablet, record your discoveries about loving your neighbor.

Group #4: Mark 12:41-44

- On a sheet of newsprint, draw an offering plate.
- Reread your passage and brainstorm ways in which we can give sacrificially to God.
- Using the Bible concordance, look up other scriptures that refer to generous giving.
- Cut out construction-paper pennies and label each one with a gift we can give to God; tape these in your offering plate.

Make necessary materials available and compare the results when the groups have finished.

Journal Meditation

Close your eyes and imagine for a moment that you are a green and leafy fig tree. Let each leaf become an object or an activity that you feel very good about or that takes a significant amount of your time and your resources. Describe or illustrate these "leaves" below.

Now imagine that Jesus comes near, brushes aside your leaves, and looks for fruit. What does he see? Is there any fruit? If so, what is the fruit? What does Jesus do? What does he say? Record your reflections below.

Stepstone to Prayer

Lord, there are mountains of difficulty in my way.
One of the largest is...

Mark 13
Trouble on the Way of the Lord

JESUS' OPPORTUNITIES FOR TEACHING HIS DISCIPLES are almost gone. In just a few days, he will be dead and buried. In this chapter, Jesus spends time alone with his disciples, giving them his last words of warning, of counsel and of encouragement. He tells them that the way they have chosen, Jesus' way, will not be an easy road to travel, but that the path has been thoroughly explored and the glorious end is sure.

This chapter, full of ominous signs and strong words of advice, may seem obscure to twentieth-century people. It is full of distinctly Jewish traditions and phrases of speech. In spite of these apparent obstacles, few chapters in this gospel are more relevant to contemporary Christians.

Jesus warns his followers to be on the alert for the many dangers of the way so that they may persevere to the end. Those who follow Jesus today know that the way has not become any easier, and that the dangers may be greater and more numerous than ever before. These verses offer us a renewed vision that will enable us to remain on Jesus' way; they instill a hope and determination that can sustain us on the perilous journey. Read MARK 13.

Find the Facts

What impressed the disciples? How will many be led astray? What signals the beginning of the birth pangs? Who will speak when the disciples are put on trial? Who will be saved? For whose sake has the Lord shortened the final days? How will the Son of man come? What will the angels do? What is Jesus' final word?

Consider:

1. Briefly list the things the disciples are told to do. Summarize what they seem to suggest about a lifestyle.

2. What feelings does this chapter evoke in you? Which images do you find the most powerful? Why?

Mark 13:1-13

A couple of things must be kept in mind as this chapter is studied. *First*, the Jews of Jesus' day had deep-seated beliefs about an event they called "the day of the Lord." This phrase referred to the time when God would break into history to establish the heavenly kingdom on earth. Through the patriarchs and prophets, God had frequently promised that a day would come when all of God's enemies would be defeated and God would reign eternally.

God's word was clear that this paradise would not come about by any human effort or institution; it would be achieved only by God's direct intervention into history. This intervention, associated with a series of terrible human disasters, cosmic shifts of stars, sun and moon, and the elimination of all that opposed God, was called "the day of the Lord" (Is. 24:21-23; Jl. 2:1-11; Am. 5:18-20).

Much literature focused on the expectation of a drastic end to this age. This literature, called *apocalyptic*, is full of visions and dreams told in highly symbolic language. No one can truly describe the events of the end of the age, but through descriptive symbols the prophets could assure the people of God's sovereign plan over history.

This chapter collects Jesus' teachings about many future events, some near to the disciples and others far from their generation. In places Jesus uses the same language associated with the prophecies of "the day of the Lord" and associates this day, the end of the age, with his second coming.

Second, these verses are full of prophecies about certain events. But Jewish prophecy, particularly apocalyptic prophecy, was never given to enable God's people to plot out a timetable of future events. The prophets' message offered God's people assurance about God's control over the apparent chaos around them.

Third, prophecy often had levels of fulfillment. A prophet would foretell a sign to the people, and the sign would come to pass. Centuries later, God's people would see that sign come to pass again in a far fuller, deeper way. This principle is true with many of Jesus' words in this chapter. Much of what he foretold has come true, yet we cannot say that it does not remain to be fulfilled again in a greater way.

In verses 1-4, Jesus' disciples comment on the magnificence of the temple. This opens the door for Jesus to talk about a variety of future events, including one as imminent as the destruction of the temple. Herod's temple, one of the wonders of the world, gleamed with gold leaf and marble brought from all over the Mediterranean. The splendor of it impressed even the jaded Romans. Yet less than 40 years after Jesus' prophecy, it lay as a pile of rubble. The temple was completely destroyed by Titus in A.D. 70 when he besieged Jerusalem and slaughtered its inhabitants.

The disciples anxiously question the timing of this destruction. Apparently they assume the destruction of the temple will coincide with the end of the age, the "day of the Lord." Jesus' response both describes the days before Jerusalem's destruction and deals with the end of the age. He spends some time discussing the dangers of deception that threaten those on the way of the Lord.

Many will be deceived by false Messiahs, leaders who claim that they are the returning Christ. Others will be led astray by the many distracting world events—wars, earthquakes and famines. But these incidents are only the beginning of labor pains; the birth of the kingdom is still in the future.

Others will be unprepared for the persecution that will pursue Jesus' followers. The communities that had welcomed them would now reject them. "Councils" and "synagogues" refers to Jewish persecution; "governors and kings" refers to the Roman source of trouble. Family ties will be broken by the disciple's new loyalty to Christ.

Jesus tells his disciples that, when their lives are on the line, they are not to give "canned" speeches. Their testimony should come out of their life experiences, from their living relationship with God. Those who are alert, ready for the suffering to come, will find the Holy Spirit filling them, enabling them to "endure to the end."

3. What seems to motivate the disciples' questions in 13:4? How do contemporary Christians deal with the desire to be in control of the future?

4. Complete this sentence: The Christian today is too impressed with the permanency of...

5. When Jesus says, "Beware" (13:5, 9), what does he mean? What are we supposed to be doing? or not doing?

Mark 13:14-23

"The desolating sacrilege" recalls a painful image from Israel's past. In the second century B.C., the Jews rebelled against their Greek conquerors because they were being forced to worship Greek gods. Antiochus Epiphanes attempted to eliminate Jewish worship by setting up a statue of Zeus in the most holy place, sacrificing pigs on the altar of Yahweh and establishing brothels in the courts. This was the "desolating sacrilege."

Jesus uses the well-understood term to describe another such desecration of God's temple (DAN. 9:27; 11:31; 12:11; 2 TH. 2:4). The time preceding it will be unequaled in its horror. Many will come pretending to be the Christ, demonstrating their power with miraculous signs. The disciples must be on their guard.

Many scholars believe these verses were fulfilled by Titus's invasion and cruel destruction of the city. Others believe these verses refer to a future event closer to the end times. Both interpretations may be correct if the prophecy has more than one level of fulfillment.

Consider:

6. Twice in this section Jesus speaks of "the elect" (13:20, 22). What clues do Jesus' words give us about the elect—their identity, their place in God's plan, etc.?

7. When have contemporary "false Messiahs and false prophets" arisen and performed miraculous signs? What has been the effect on God's people? How can we discern the truth about these deceivers?

Mark 13:24-27

The "birth pangs" that Jesus refers to in verse 8 will culminate in the shifting and the disarming of cosmic forces. This description of the solar and lunar eclipses and the falling stars again draws on typical apocalyptic imagery. These images connote more than mere physical, astronomical events.

The people of Jesus' day believed that the celestial bodies were visual symbols of unseen spiritual powers, not necessarily benevolent to human beings. The shaking of "the powers in the heavens" becomes visible in these outward changes. The "Son of man" does the shaking; he upsets the spiritual authorities who persecute God's people. The early Church identified this celestial "Son" prophesied by Daniel (DAN. 7:13-14) with the glorified Christ who will return to earth in power and glory with clouds of angels surrounding him.

The whole New Testament is full of this expectation. In the early Church, the hope of the second coming ignited the faith of the believers and gave them courage in desperate times. In the Church today, perhaps because of the arrogance of those who wish to calculate the days and times of Jesus' return, many in disgust have lost their expectation of Christ's cosmic victory.

Nevertheless, human apathy will not change God's plans. This must again become the battle cry of the Church. God, not human effort, will bring the defeat of evil. Jesus calls his followers to live in light of this promise, waiting expectantly for the Son of man to appear in glory.

8. Reread 13:1-27 carefully and list the major events described. What are your general conclusions about the future? Why is it significant to you to know that history is going somewhere?

9. Read Daniel 7:13-14, Isaiah 11:12 and Zephaniah 3:19-20. What new insights do these prophecies give to your understanding of Jesus' words?

Mark 13:28-37

When the fig tree sends out its green and tender new branches, summer is near. So it is with God's movements in history. Jesus' lesson in verses 28-31 concerns the more imminent fate of Jerusalem, an event that would take place in the lifetime of the disciples' generation. Jesus knows how close that incident is. He does not, however, know when the end of the world will come (13:32), an event that lies in the timing and control of the Father.

Because Jesus' disciples are not given timetables for the future, they must stay alert. This is the core of Jesus' message about the future. Do not occupy yourselves, Jesus says, with calculations and predictions and anxiety, but "keep alert," "keep awake" (13:33, 35, 37). Jesus is going away and, like the master of the house, has put his servants in charge until he returns. He will return. Christians are the doorkeepers who stand guard through the dark hours of the night, ready to welcome the master home.

Consider:

10. Is constant vigilance possible? Why or why not? What do you think being "asleep" when the Lord returns means (13:36)? Would you say you are watchful or sleepy?

11. List the practical implications that Jesus' teaching suggests for his disciples. For each implication, consider what you are going to do or change to accomplish that implication.

12. In what ways might Jesus' words in verses 35-37 also apply to the Lord's "return" at the end of our lives or at the end of a time of personal difficulty when God seems far away?

Group Activities

1. Divide into groups of three or four and discuss the following questions:
   - What clues does Jesus give in this chapter about the specific behaviors that a watchful attitude might involve?
   - Which of these behaviors occupy the Church today?
   - Which of these behaviors are present in your life?
   - Why do contemporary Christians fail to watch?
   - What are obstacles to watching?
   - How can the Church recover its watchful attitude?

   Reassemble the group and compare findings. Ask for a volunteer to read aloud 1 THESSALONIANS 4:13-28. Spend a few moments in silent prayer; then close by inviting group members to pray aloud for the Church to prepare for Jesus' return.

2. Brainstorm together a list of emotions and thoughts people might have as they go through the end times. Record group members' responses in a column on chalkboard, whiteboard or newsprint. In a second column record answers to the following questions:
   - What other emotions and thoughts might Christians have as they go through the end times?

- What emotions and thoughts do you think Jesus expects his followers to have when they go through the end times?

Compare the lists and respond to the following question:
- What benefit will there be for Jesus' followers during the traumatic times before his return?

3. Distribute drawing paper and crayons. Ask each group member to reread MARK 13, choose one image that has especially affected him or her in some way, and illustrate that image. They may wish to illustrate the specific event literally or symbolically, or they may choose to illustrate their impressions or emotions of that event.

Invite volunteers to share their drawings with the group and to explain their choices.

Journal Meditation

Reread MARK 13:5-8. Quietly consider for a few moments the current international news. Where are the "birth pangs" most painfully present in the world today? In what ways can you perceive the kingdom of God being born around the world?

In the space below, describe the way you feel about the evidence, or seeming lack of evidence, of God's control in the world today.

Stepstone to Prayer

Lord, I know that even in view of these world events, my personal faithfulness and watchfulness are of great importance to you. Help me to...

Mark 14
The Way of Courage and Suffering

IN THIS CHAPTER, MARK WEAVES TOGETHER a number of narrative strands into a dark tapestry of betrayal, denial and abandonment. His followers witness the collapse of the kingdom that they had anticipated for years. Even the disciples—Jesus' most intimate and faithful friends—flee in disappointment, fright and confusion. Yet Jesus continues down the inexorable path to the cross, a witness to faith in God and in God's plan for creation.

Christians today play a key role in that plan. This horrible final week of Jesus' life is made horrible for God's people. Through the ominous tapestry runs a thread of love and hope. That thread—the coming of salvation and peace for all believers—weaves today's people of God into the same tapestry. *We* become a part of this passion week narrative: our fear reflects the disciples' fear, our denial of Jesus echoes Peter's denial and our flight from Jesus' pain traces the steps of the fleeing disciples. Mark invites us to experience these dark moments, to gaze with awe at the tapestry of our deliverance in these final chapters of his gospel. Read MARK 14.

Find the Facts

When do these events take place? What does the woman do for Jesus? What deal does Judas make with the chief priests? What announcement does Jesus make during the Passover? What does Jesus say will happen to his followers? to Peter? What does Jesus do in Gethsemane? In what way does Jesus identify himself before the high priest? How many times does Peter deny Jesus?

Consider:

1. List the individuals and groups mentioned in Mark 14. At the conclusion of Mark 14, what do you imagine each person or group is thinking? feeling? fearing? hoping?

2. For each person or group listed in question 1, write a contemporary example of a similar person or group. In what ways do these contemporary persons or groups help the spread of God's kingdom? hinder the spread of the kingdom?

Mark 14:1-11

Jerusalem fills with pilgrims from around the world during the annual celebration of Passover. Visitors occupy every available room. Those packing the city include zealots, national fanatics fomenting for rebellion against Rome.

The Jewish religious leaders identify Jesus as one such dissident, and, consequently, as a threat to the established balance of Roman and Jewish power. For the sake of peace, Jesus must be removed and killed. Yet, because of Jesus' popularity, his arrest might provoke a riot. Any move against him must proceed cautiously and secretly.

Jesus, meanwhile, spends the last evening before his trial at the home of Simon, a cured leper. During dinner, indicative of fellowship and acceptance, an anonymous woman arrives with a carved, alabaster jar filled with costly "nard" or "spikenard," fragrant ointment made from an eastern plant. The woman illustrates the solemn character of the moment and the uniqueness of Jesus' person as she anoints Jesus' head, declaring her love for this man who has brought her the joy of God's forgiveness.

Others express a different view of the woman's offering. They see the gift as a waste. From a utilitarian point of view, the cost of the perfume, a year's labor, could have been used to alleviate the suffering of the poor. A *denarii* was the normal wage for a day. Jesus' response points out an important truth about sacrifice and worship: there are times when the simple and pure worship of Jesus outweighs even the pressing needs of the poor. These interruptions in the normal responsibility for the poor are valid only on special occasions of worship. Love does not only do good things; at times it does lovely things without counting the cost.

The anointing mentioned by Jesus refers to the Jewish custom of bathing the dead body and perfuming it before burial. Consciously, this may not have been the woman's intent. Jesus, however, points out the meaning for the other dinner guests; the woman's action foreshadows his approaching death.

Jesus' attitude toward this extravagant gift seems to irritate Judas to the point that he does something he has probably been contemplating for some time: Judas decides to collaborate with the Jewish authorities. When Judas realizes that Jesus' pathway differs from his own vision, he may believe that he can bring about Jesus' national leadership by setting up a conflict between Jesus and the authorities, a conflict forcing Jesus to save himself and establish, finally and literally, Judas's vision of the kingdom of God. The evangelist Matthew tells of Judas's later remorse; apparently Judas's plan, whatever it was, backfired (MT. 27:1-5).

Consider:

3. Name some "good services" done in the name of Jesus that some may label a waste. When have you felt as indignant as the disciples? When have you wanted to be as lavish in your worship of Jesus as is the woman in this story? In what ways might the Church "count the cost" too carefully when trying to honor Christ?

4. Describe some good thing you have done that God later showed had a larger meaning or result. What does this indicate to you about God's active presence in your life?

5. When have you attempted to force God's hand to accomplish something you thought most important? What were the results? In what areas of your life today do you most need patience with God?

Mark 14:12-25

Surely Jesus' betrayal by one of his close disciples is among the lowest points in his life. Judas's desire to control Jesus stands in stark contrast with the anointing of the adoring woman, who wants to give all that she can to Jesus out of gratitude and devotion.

These verses introduce another painful and dramatic contrast: Here at the table, surrounded by his friends, Jesus initiates the eucharist, the most intimate symbol of the Christian faith, while in the same dipping of the bread he identifies the one who betrays him. It is not the opposition to Jesus' truth that proves to be the most serious enemy, but the betrayal that comes from the inner circle of followers. Nor is it Judas alone who must question his loyalty; each disciple pauses to ask, "Surely, not I?" (14:19).

The betrayal occurs during the joint celebration of the old covenant and the institution of the new. The new covenant, communion with God through Christ, grows out of the Jewish Passover. The whole history of Israel—the rebellious people of God encountering the love of God—is summed up by the startling blending of these two events—Judas's betrayal and Jesus' celebration of the Passover.

In this final Passover meal, Jesus demonstrates in tangible signs that God's love continues in the face of abandonment and denial. Judas may betray, Peter may deny, and all others may flee, but the promises of God remain. God's people may turn away, but God nonetheless pours out good gifts, the gifts of Jesus' body and blood.

The symbols of the Passover meal were reminders of past bondage and deliverance, finding their fulfillment in the life and death of Jesus. The innocent Passover lamb gave its life so that the people were "passed over," delivered from death (Ex. 12:1-36).

After the Israelites escaped from Egypt and reached the promised land, the worshiper would bring a lamb during Passover and offer it for sacrifice. After the lamb was killed, the priests splashed its blood—the symbol of life—on the altar, and the lamb was given back to the worshiper for a feast. From the sacrifice of the lamb came the forgiveness of sin, the restoration of the relationship with God, and a powerful reminder of God's faithful deliverance from bondage in Egypt.

In Christ, the same God delivers the world out of its bondage to sin. God sacrifices Jesus as the ultimate offering for sin, then returns him to believers in the eucharist as the continuing feast of the Christian life, a celebration that lasts through eternity.

Consider:

6. In the old covenant, God promised to guide and protect the people of Israel. In return, Israel promised to obey God and worship God alone. Compare this with the new covenant established by Jesus in Mark 14:22-25. What does Jesus promise in the new covenant? What is expected of the disciples? From this comparison, what conclusions can you draw about God's plan for humanity? for you?

7. Even with the knowledge that Judas has betrayed him, Jesus includes him in the eucharist, sharing his most intimate gift to the disciples. What would you have done had you been Jesus? Why do you think Jesus allows Judas to remain? What does this indicate to you about God?

8. What do you think Jesus offers us in his body and blood? List all that you receive when you receive the eucharist.

Mark 14:26-52

The Mount of Olives sits across a little valley called Kidron on the east side of Jerusalem. The Garden of Gethsemane lies a little way up the hillside. Jesus probably visited the garden frequently to spend time in prayer away from the city.

Jesus warns his disciples of the confusion and fear that will very soon beset them all. He knows they will desert him, and he wants them to know that he knows. Their unfaithfulness will not take him by surprise, nor will it change his plan to be reunited with them after he has risen.

Peter boasts of his courage and fidelity, but Jesus is not persuaded. Peter's denials will be the most emphatic. Nevertheless, Jesus invites his disciples' prayer and includes Peter, along with James and John, in his most painful moments before God.

This moment in Mark's passion narrative reveals the heart of Jesus' relationship with his Father. This struggle in the garden is not a sham. Some part of Jesus resists what he knows is ahead if the betrayers' plan succeeds. Jesus does not want to die. Yet, though his soul is sorrowful, he wants to be obedient to the Father, even when obedience points in the direction of the cross.

Jesus wrestles with his decision. Three times he prays, falling to the ground in weakness. He makes every effort to steel his mind and solidify his resolve. He searches for another way. At the end of his prayer time, he knows that this is God's will. He will trust the Father even if he does not fully understand.

The disciples cannot share his struggle. The conflict ahead does not seem to agonize them as it does Jesus. Their spirits are loyal, but their flesh falls asleep, runs away and denies Jesus.

Judas is more alert than the others. He has been busy gathering the temple authorities and now he presides over the official arrest. A kiss, the sign Judas agreed to give to the Sanhedrin, is a normal way to greet an honored rabbi. Judas betrays his Lord with a show of deep affection. Jesus submits to the arrest, though he protests the cowardice and underhanded attitude that leads the authorities to arrest an unarmed, non-violent man with "swords and clubs" in the dead of night. Even so, Jesus knows that scripture foretold even this:

> "Awake, O sword, against my shepherd,
>   against the man who is my associate,"
>   says the Lord of hosts.
> Strike the shepherd, that the sheep may be scattered (ZECH. 13:7).

9. List the different issues with which you think Jesus is struggling as he prays in the garden. How are these or similar issues involved in your most difficult decisions?

10. Since the disciples knew that Jesus would soon be betrayed and arrested, why do you think sleep overcame the disciples? When have you felt the same inability to "keep awake and pray"? What are some remedies for such spiritual inertia?

11. What does the entire scene in the garden—from Jesus' time in prayer to his apparent readiness to rise and meet his betrayer—indicate about Jesus' relationship with the Father? Would you say your relationship with God is at all similar? Why or why not?

Mark 14:53-72

The council before which Jesus stands did not have the power to execute criminals. Instead, it prepared charges that, by law, required a trial before the Roman governor.

When Jesus finally answers the High Priest's question, he exhibits great courage. Jesus knows that his answer will bring his death, for he does not hesitate to claim to be the Anointed One of God, who is on intimate terms with God and who will reign in glory (Ps. 110:1; Dan. 7:13). On anyone else's lips, this claim would indeed have been blasphemous. Jesus' mission, however, so powerfully manifested in all that he had said and done over the last three years, proved that he alone could say this truthfully. Jesus' courage reveals an incredible confidence that the Father will one day demonstrate the Lordship and divinity of the Son and fulfill all that Jesus had begun.

Peter seems to want to be near, though he makes no move to intervene in the proceedings or defend Jesus before the council. He hovers in the courtyard of the high priest's house, perhaps waiting for Jesus' release.

As the situation gets more tense, Peter feels more threatened. Within a few hours, he denies three times that he has any connection with Jesus. When he remembers that Jesus had told him this would happen, he breaks down and cries in a profound demonstration of grief, confession and repentance. Much later in his life, Peter finds himself in an even more menacing situation when he is associated with "the man from Nazareth." Then he would courageously die for his Lord, empowered by his painful experience of Jesus' faithfulness in spite of Peter's weakness.

12. Why do you think Jesus keeps silent for part of the trial, but later speaks up? List the things that Jesus' simple claim indicates about his true identity, the future and the Father's attitude toward Jesus.

13. Review Peter's role in Mark 14. What did he say and to whom? How does Peter's denial of Jesus differ from Judas's betrayal? What does this suggest about Judas's relationship with Jesus? Peter's relationship with Jesus?

14. When have you denied Jesus? When have you run from an opportunity to announce that you were a follower of Jesus? What motivated the denial? the running? When have you stood up for Jesus in the face of possible persecution? What motivated your stand?

Group Activities

1. Before meeting, gather information about the Jewish Passover meal, the Seder. Include an explanation of the meaning of each element of the Seder dinner. If possible, set up the room with low tables and cushions and arrange for the use of another room to represent Gethsemane and a third room to represent the high priest's house.

   In your group, assign the parts of the *disciples, the crowd, the high priest, the false witnesses* and *Jesus*, and reenact MARK 14:17-72. Ask a narrator to read the descriptive portions, pausing to give characters time to read their parts and perform their actions. Encourage ad-libbing. In conclusion, ask:
   - What were you feeling during our drama?
   - What did you learn about your character?
   - What would you like to ask about the other characters?

2. Discuss together the tapestry imagery of the introduction to this study (p. 122). Invite group members to reflect on the various strands woven throughout MARK 14. Ask:
   - Which story touches you personally? Why?
   - Which story reflects your Christian experience?

   Distribute paper and pencils. Invite each group member to draw parallels between the elements in one of the stories of MARK 14 to elements in an experience from their own lives. Ask volunteers to share their comparisons with the group.

3. Divide group members into groups of three or four. Distribute paper and pencils to groups. Ask each group to write a brief statement to Jesus for each of the scenes in MARK 14. What would they like to say to Jesus on each stop of this painful path?

   Gather group members and invite them to use their statements as today's closing prayer.

Journal Meditation

Recall some of the darkest moments of your life, times when you struggled with God's will and with the prospect of great suffering. Were you spiritually watchful or asleep? Why?

Spend a few moments listing your fears for the future. Now reread MARK 14:37-38. What temptations do those fears represent? In what ways can you watch and pray? How can you strengthen the flesh to correspond with the willingness of your spirit? Record your reflections below.

Stepstone to Prayer

Lord, I do not want to deny you. Instead of running from conflict, help me to...

Mark 15:1-41
The Way of the Cross

ESUS STANDS ALONE AT THE CENTER of an intensifying storm of deceit and danger. Like a lightning rod he draws to himself the world's hatred. In contrast to Jesus' calm, pure spirit, the world's anger—violent, self-serving and hypocritical—stands out in sharp relief. The events of this chapter reveal humanity's desperate need for the salvation God brings through Jesus Christ.

The people who take part in these events represent every segment of society. Jesus faces the unjust accusations of the religious leaders, lawyers, courts and counselors—those empowered to lead the people into righteousness and justice. He withstands the attacks of political leaders and the military—those who supposedly work for peace. He is rejected by criminals, ordinary citizens and bystanders—those to whom he had reached out in love and healing. He feels the faithlessness of friends and disciples—those with whom he had walked, talked and lived. All people crucify the love of God incarnate in Jesus. Read MARK 15:1-41.

Find the Facts

By whom is Jesus questioned? Why is Barabbas released instead of Jesus? How is Jesus treated by the soldiers? by the robbers? by those who pass by the cross? by the priests and teachers? by those who crucify him? What does Jesus say from the cross? What events accompany his death? Where is Jesus buried and by whom?

Consider:

1. *Complete this sentence: Jesus dies on the cross because...*

2. *Complete this sentence: When Jesus dies on the cross, he reveals...*

Mark 15:1-5

The council reconvenes to confirm the decision made the night before: Jesus is guilty of blasphemy and must die. The authorities deliver Jesus to Pilate because they do not have the legal right to execute the penalty of death. But a charge of blasphemy is a religious accusation and will not bring the death penalty in a court of Roman law. The Jewish leaders translate the charge of blasphemy into one of sedition against Rome: "Jesus calls himself the 'King of the Jews'. There can be no king but Caesar!" (LK. 23:1-2; JN. 19:12-16). Jesus' accusers twist his claim to be the Messiah (14:61-62) into a political claim to be the King of Israel and thus a threat to Rome's authority. Jesus' enigmatic answer to Pilate's interrogation neither confirms nor denies Pilate's fears about a military insurrection. Though Jesus did not come to set up a political reign (JN. 18:33-37), his kingship would indeed rock the Roman empire, transforming lives and conquering evil in every segment of the society.

Nevertheless, Pilate recognizes the falseness of the charges. He understands that Jesus represents no political or military threat to Rome. His own spies have told him the facts. Pilate knows that the chief priests are motivated by envy rather than by the piety and political loyalty they feign. Thus he is amazed at Jesus' silence: Why does this man not answer his accusers? Perhaps Jesus' silence pictures God's revealing silence in the face of sin and falsehood.

Consider:

3. Why do you think Jesus' response to Pilate is not more direct? What point is Jesus making? Speculate on what might have happened had Jesus said "Yes" or "No."

4. When have you been falsely accused of something at work? at home? with friends? How have you responded to your accusers? What defense have you made? To what extent can we leave vindication in God's hands?

Mark 15:6-20

It is possible that many in Jerusalem regarded Barabbas as a hero. Though history shrouds his identity, he likely fought with the Zealots to overthrow Rome. At some point in the recent past he had led a bloody insurrection. The choice of Barabbas over Jesus betrays the people's self-interest. They choose a man of violence and vengeance instead of a man of healing and acceptance. They want vindication, not redemption. They want supremacy, not a new relationship with God. They choose the way of hatred, not the way of love. They choose physical force and tyranny, not forgiveness and peace.

In Pilate, political expediency takes precedence over justice and integrity. In order to avoid responsibility for the decision, Pilate shifts the choice to the people, assuming that Jesus' obvious innocence will cause them to choose Jesus.

The chief priests, meanwhile, take advantage of the lowest impulses of the people to protect their power and privilege. Like an evil earthquake (the Greek root for "stirred up," v. 11), they rumble through the crowd, inciting them to choose Barabbas, until the cry breaks open against Jesus, "Crucify him!" Fairness and truth sink below the surface of the crowd's hatred of Rome. The chief priests manipulate while Pilate capitulates—both for self-serving reasons.

The soldiers also turn against Jesus in a display of brutal humor. Their mocking worship of him makes use of a purple robe, a color suggesting royalty; a ring of briers, suggesting a crown; an exaggerated salutation similar to that offered to Caesar; and spitting, perhaps a parody of the common kiss of homage offered to eastern royalty.

5. Compare the crowd that accompanied Jesus into Jerusalem (11:8-10) with this crowd (15:6-15). Why do you think they respond so differently to Jesus? What varying responses to Jesus have you experienced in your spiritual journey? What does this say about human nature? about God's love?

6. Describe your emotional response to the soldiers' mistreatment of Jesus. In what ways is Jesus mocked and mistreated today? In what ways does the Church respond to the contemporary mistreatment of Jesus?

7. Read John 18:28–19:16. Consider Pilate's dilemma. What do you think he could have, or should have, done? What would have been the results? In what ways was he God's instrument for the fulfilling of God's purposes?

8. When have you been faced with a choice of expedience over integrity? What empowers you to face up to the disapproval of "the crowds"?

Mark 15:21-32

What bad luck for Simon, a Jewish pilgrim from North Africa in Jerusalem for the Passover—an innocent bystander shouldered with the gruesome task of carrying a cross for a crucifixion. Was Simon in the wrong place at the wrong time? The fact that Mark includes the names of Simon's sons suggests that perhaps the incident did more than cause Simon to curse his luck.

Apparently Simon's sons were later known to the Christian community and may, in fact, have become personal friends of the apostle Paul (ROM. 16:13). What happens to Simon at the foot of the cross he carries to Golgotha? Perhaps as Simon walks the way of the cross with Jesus, he becomes the model disciple who "takes up his cross and follows Jesus" (8:34).

At Golgotha the soldiers crucify Jesus. Crucifixion was both an agonizing and humiliating method of execution. Usually reserved for slaves and the worst of offenders, crucifixion began by nailing the victim's heels and wrists to a cross. The cross was then quickly raised and suddenly dropped into a crudely dug hole.

A crucified victim could suffer excruciating pain for several days before life gave out. Death usually occurred from suffocation. As the victim became more tired, he would no longer be able to push up on his legs and raise his chest to breathe. If life lingered and the soldiers wished to hasten death, they would break the victim's legs, thereby assuring a speedy suffocation.

According to tradition, compassionate women from Jerusalem often offered a mixture of wine and myrrh to dying criminals. The wine and myrrh combined to produce an anesthetic, thus relieving the suffering of the dying. Jesus refuses it.

Crucifixions ranked low on a Roman soldier's list of favorite assignments. For this reason, the minor possessions of the condemned became "bonus pay" for the soldiers. Thus the soldiers divide Jesus' garments among themselves. Mark's account points out that every detail of Jesus' death points to Jesus' true identity.

For dogs are all around me;
    a company of evildoers encircles me;
My hands and feet have shriveled;
I can count all my bones.
They stare and gloat over me;
    they divide my clothes among themselves,
and for my clothing they cast lots (Ps. 22:16-18).

In accordance with the tradition of listing the charges brought against the victim, the plaque placed above Jesus' head tells the world that this man is the King of the Jews. The wording of the charge shows Pilate's anger and mockery of the Jewish authorities and their hypocrisy. Instead of crucifying an imposter who *claimed* to be the King of the Jews, Pilate actually crucifies their King (JN. 19:19-22). No one understood then how true Pilate's final statement really was.

The chief priests continue to be involved in every step of Jesus' assassination. They leave nothing to chance, so much do they hate and fear him. "Save yourself," they mock. But Jesus cannot save himself, not if he truly embodies the nature and love of God. Because Jesus does not come down from the cross, he makes Christian faith possible.

If Jesus were to quit the cross short of tasting the bottom of the cup, he would tell the world that God's love has a limit, a point past which the Creator will not suffer in order to love us. Because Jesus suffers and dies, Christians see the cross and say, "God loves us that much."

Consider:

9. *How do you imagine Simon responds to the command to carry Jesus' cross? What thoughts might Simon have? What events of the crucifixion may have led to Simon's conversion?*

10. Why do you think Jesus refuses to drink the drugged wine? What does this suggest to you about the nature of ministry in today's Church?

11. Why do you think Mark mentions that Jesus was crucified between two robbers? Why is this final humiliation appropriate in view of Jesus' ministry to the common people?

12. Imagine Jesus' response to each of the statements made in his hearing as he hung on the cross. What different meanings do you hear in each statement said to or about him?

Mark 15:33-41

At noon, when daylight should shine most brightly, an unnatural darkness shrouds Israel. It is a dark hour for God's people, a low point in their relationship to their Creator. It is a darkness that belongs to all of humanity, not just the Jews. It is a darkness owned by all people throughout all time. The murder of the Son of God is so unnatural that nature itself loses its light.

"My God, my God," cries Jesus, quoting the first verse of PSALM 22 to express the alienation he feels from his Father. Sin alienates all people from God. He who had never sinned and hence never experienced separation from the Father suffers the depths of the human condition—separation from the Source of life. Here Jesus reaches his final level of identification with humanity. He enters into and experiences sin. God now goes to the limit in loving humankind, beyond suffering to the separation caused by sin.

The temple curtain mentioned in verse 38 hung between the holy place and the most holy place. God was thought to dwell as a shining light within the most holy place. The curtain symbolized the people's inability to encounter God directly; God's holiness and humanity's sinfulness could not meet or God's fiery purity would extinguish fleshly lives.

As Jesus relinquishes his final breath, loving humanity completely, all barriers between God and God's people—real or imagined—rip apart. The curtain tears from top to bottom, not from below, by human effort, but from above, as God clears the way to the most holy place, making it possible to come immediately and without fear into God's presence (HEB. 9:8-12; 10:19-22). God banishes obscurity and cowering. All is open. God's people no longer guess or grope when seeking the face of God. They see God's face in the face of the crucified Christ.

The centurion, a commander of 100 Roman soldiers, stares open-mouthed at the lifeless body of Jesus hanging on the cross. He does not see another dead insurrectionist; he sees the Son of God. Mark includes this confession by the hardened centurion as testimony to the dramatic impact Jesus' suffering and death has on those who witness it. Even the centurion believes.

Mark also mentions several women by name. In this Mark honors the loyalty of these women. The male followers of Jesus flee. The women remain with him as he dies.

And so the storm that envelops Jesus on this awful day finally begins to die. The moans of the dying fade. The jeering stops. Dusk approaches. The Son of God hangs dead on the cross.

13. Read Psalm 22 and note how many confident statements are made by the psalmist. Why do you think Jesus quotes from this psalm? What might Jesus have been telling those who were witnessing his crucifixion? What might Jesus have been telling God? What does this say to you?

14. What barriers exist in your relationship with God? What effect do these barriers have in your spiritual life? your life with others? What has God done to remove these barriers? What can you do to further remove these barriers?

15. The centurion responds to the events of Mark 15 with, "Truly this man was God's Son!" What is your personal response to Jesus' trial, crucifixion and death?

16. Why do you think the women assemble at the crucifixion while the men avoid the scene? Had you been one of Jesus' followers during his earthly ministry, would you have remained with him to the end? Explain your answer.

Group Activities

1. On newsprint, whiteboard or chalkboard copy this list of people involved in the story of Jesus' trial and crucifixion:
   - religious leaders
   - politicians
   - the military
   - ordinary citizens/bystanders
   - nationalists/terrorists
   - criminals
   - friends/disciples

   Distribute issues of recent newspapers and news magazines. Ask each group member to choose one of the groups of people on the list. Offer these directions:
   - Find an article or photograph that is about the contemporary equivalent of the people in the group that you chose.
   - Evaluate the actions of those in the article or photo. In what ways are they behaving like their counterparts in Mark 15?
   - In what way is the crucifixion of Jesus Christ repeated in the article or photo you chose?

   Invite volunteers to share their findings.

2. Invite group members to sit in an alert but relaxed position with eyes closed. Dramatically read aloud Mark 15:1-34. Follow verse 34, which quotes Psalm 22:1, with the rest of Psalm 22, reading slowly and thoughtfully. (If time allows, follow the reading of Psalm 22 with Isaiah 53.)

   Continue by reading Mark 15:35-39. Pause for silent meditation at the end.

   After several minutes, invite group members to open their eyes. Let them share their thoughts and feelings if they wish.

3. Divide group members into small groups of three or four. Give each group a blank piece of poster board and several colored felt markers. Invite each group to discuss and create a poster reflecting the group members' response to Mark 15:1-41. Offer no further guidelines. When groups have finished, invite them to share their finished posters with other groups.

Journal Meditation

You stand at the foot of the cross. You hear the pounding of nails and the groaning of men. The soldiers raise the three crucified men. The sun goes dim. Listen! What are people saying to Jesus? to each other? to you? Look! What do you see as you look into the face of the dying Jesus? Speak! What do you say to your Savior?

Stepstone to Prayer

Lord Jesus, thank you for your obedience to your Father. Thank you for that incredible love. In response, I...

Mark 15:42–16:20
The Way of the Resurrection

DARK AND PAINFUL AS THE EVENTS OF JESUS' ARREST, trial, crucifixion and death seemed to his disciples, the ultimate crisis for God's great creation still had to be faced. The darkness of the tomb forces the disciples to face their own mortality. Is death the end? Is there no cause for hope?

If Jesus, the human incarnation of God, dies and stays dead, then death is the ultimate fact of the universe. Everything decays and runs down. All things fade and die. Death wins; grace, truth, peace, hope and love lose. Creation lives to die

But if Jesus comes alive from the dead, he proclaims the truth of irresistible life beyond the grave, life that reveals the depths of the creative heart of God. The God who loved, healed and forgave in Jesus triumphs over death and reigns forever, more powerful than any force in the universe.

We face the same dilemma today. The rationalistic society in which we live would have us believe that death is the end, that we have no reason to hope for (or to fear) a bigger, better life with God after this one. Jesus' resurrection challenges us, as it did his disciples, to believe, to hope, to face the future, including our own deaths, with confidence. Read MARK 15:42–16:20.

Find the Facts

Who arranges for Jesus' burial? Who else witnesses the burial? Who comes to the tomb early on Sunday morning? What do they see? What is their response? How do the disciples react when told of Jesus' resurrection? to whom does Jesus appear? What does Jesus tell his disciples to do? Where does Jesus go after commissioning the disciples?

Consider:

1. Which words or phrases most dramatically communicate to you the wonder of the resurrection? Why?

2. With whom in these stories do you most identify? Explain your answer.

Mark 15:42-47

Jesus dies at 3 o'clock on Friday afternoon. He had hung on the cross for six hours before dying, a short time compared to many crucifixions. This is perhaps understandable considering the inner turmoil Jesus had been facing as he contemplated his own death, his resolute decision to submit to death, the beatings by the temple guards (14:65) and the Roman soldiers (15:19), and the severe scourging ordered by Pilate (15:15). A Roman scourging was often fatal.

At 6 o'clock in the evening, the Sabbath would begin. The author of the Gospel of John tells us that the Jews were anxious that the bodies of the criminals be removed before the Sabbath began. In response to their request, Pilate orders the legs of the criminals broken to speed their death (JN. 19:31-34). The bodies of executed criminals were usually tossed into a pauper's field unless a close relative requested otherwise.

Mark's seemingly casual mention of Joseph of Arimathea deserves note. Here is a rich and respected member of the council, a courageous man who "had not agreed to (the council's) plan and action" (LK. 23:51). Joseph does the unthinkable. He associates himself openly and decisively with Jesus by asking Pilate if he could have the body of Jesus to bury before the Sabbath began.

It would have been easy for Joseph to grieve privately for Jesus and keep his opinions to himself. After all, Jesus was dead. What is the point in this blunt challenge to his peers in the council? Mark tells us that Joseph was "waiting expectantly for the kingdom of God." Perhaps Joseph saw a glimpse of the kingdom there on the cross. We do not know if he hoped for a resurrection, but clearly Joseph feels there is a good reason even now to walk in Jesus' way.

3. What does Joseph's action say about his discipleship? What do you think motivates Joseph to publicize his loyalty to Jesus by giving him a decent burial?

4. What kind of person today looks for the kingdom of God? In what ways are you looking? What do you expect to see?

5. Imagine the thoughts of the other members of the council when they hear of Joseph's act. How do you think they feel toward Joseph? How do you think they feel about Jesus' honored burial?

Mark 16:1-8

The women who love Jesus are hindered by the Sabbath regulations from bringing spices for the body of Jesus. They come as early as they can to do their duty. The Jews did not embalm their dead, but they would honor their loved ones by mourning over the body, anointing it with oils and wrapping it in spices.

The women come filled with a sense of loss and grief for the one they love. In their sorrow, they fail to plan for the biggest obstacle to their mourning: the stone in front of the tomb. The tomb was carved out of rock; in front of the opening, a deep groove had been chiseled to hold a large wheel of stone. It would take several men to roll the stone into place, but the women went with their spices and perfume without making arrangements for a way to enter the tomb.

When they look up, they find their way clear. Perhaps they think someone else has the same idea about anointing Jesus' body. But when they enter the tomb, they encounter a stranger, a "young man, dressed in a white robe." Clearly this person is no ordinary person, or the women would not be "amazed." The author of the Gospel of Matthew identifies this messenger as an angel of the Lord (Mt. 28:2-4) and the author of the Gospel of Luke says that the man's clothing was "dazzling" (Lk. 24:4).

The messenger's announcement is that Jesus lives; Jesus is not a dead teacher to be quoted nor a martyred prophet to be enshrined. He is someone to talk to, not just talk about. The other gospel writers tell of several immediate appearances of Jesus to various disciples; for Mark, the empty tomb is the most dramatic and convincing evidence of the great miracle.

The messenger commissions the women to tell the "disciples and Peter" the good news of Jesus' resurrection and his desire to meet with them. Surely the disciples would wonder if Jesus would want to see them again. Jesus' message reminds them that Jesus had known all that would happen, including their abandonment, and that the fellowship between them is not broken (16:7; 14:28). Jesus' special reference to Peter apart from the other disciples would reassure him that Jesus still loves and accepts him, though Peter surely feels great remorse and shame.

Galilee is the disciples' home base. It is natural for them to return to the familiar and the common. From the tomb of death comes the announcement that the living Christ will meet his friends in the familiar and routine places and events of their lives. The resurrected Jesus transforms the ordinary into new and fresh channels of encounter with God.

The women are frightened and confused, trembling with an astonishment that borders on panic. They say nothing about this strange encounter and announcement at the tomb. Their silence invites the reader to proclaim the good news. Unfortunately, many Christians today say nothing about the most inspiring, astonishing and affirming fact in the whole universe.

Consider:

6. Read Acts 2:22-24. Why was it "impossible for him to be held" by death? Why did early Christians believe that Jesus' resurrection was irresistible and inevitable?

7. In what ways do you think the Church does today what the women set out to do, that is, to perfume and preserve a dead body? What should we be doing instead? What duties do we perform that can turn into life-changing surprises? When has this happened to you?

8. What do you think the women's anxiety over the stone barrier might represent in the Church today? What obstacles do we mistakenly assume keep us from God? When have you wanted to do something for God but have been worried about some hurdle to be overcome?

9. Reread Mark 16:7, putting your name in place of Peter's. In what ways have you, like Peter, denied your relationship with Jesus? How has this caused you to doubt God's love for you? What does Jesus' message say to you?

Mark 16:9-18

Most scholars believe that the original Gospel of Mark ended at verse 8 or that the original ending has been lost. A careful reading of verses 9-20 shows how different it is from the body of the gospel. Apparently a faithful Christian later wrote and appended verses 9-20 to the gospel in order to summarize the true disciple's experience and the call of Jesus to the Church. Though it may not be written by Mark, we can assume that the Holy Spirit who oversaw the composition of the gospel thought it valuable for our instruction.

Mary Magdalene had been freed from many demons by Jesus at some point in his ministry (LK. 8:2), and in gratitude she followed Jesus throughout his ministry, caring for his needs (15:40-41). She kept watch at the cross during his gruesome death and now becomes the first witness to the resurrected Jesus. Mary does not keep the news to herself. She stubbornly proclaims that Jesus lives, though the disciples do not believe it.

Verse 12 refers to Luke's story of the two travelers on the road to Emmaus (LK. 24:13-35). Their witness is also rejected. Finally Jesus appears to the eleven remaining disciples (Judas having committed suicide) and gently chides them for "their lack of faith and stubbornness." They had willfully rejected the good news, and Jesus calls them to open their eyes and hearts and accept the gospel. Only the believing and tenderhearted will have the power to penetrate the world with the gospel. Only the believing can speak to "the whole creation."

In verses 16-18, Jesus gives the Church, the assembly of Jesus' followers, its message—salvation comes through faith and baptism; its authority—over every form of evil, physical or spiritual, and over every barrier; and its mission—to heal the sick.

Consider:

10. Why do you think Jesus chooses Mary Magdalene to be his first witness? What does this communicate to the Church today about Jesus' priorities?

11. Why do the disciples persist in unbelief? What causes unbelief? What causes belief?

12. Compare 16:16 with John 3:16-18. What is salvation? What is condemnation? Why do you think God gives us the power to choose?

13. How well do you think the Church is proclaiming the message? exercising its authority? fulfilling its mission? Explain your answer.

Mark 16:19-20

In fulfillment of Jesus' one quiet statement to the high priest (14:62), Jesus returns to the Father and sits down at God's right hand. Such a position bespeaks the authority and glory due to Jesus (Ps. 110:1). It also offers a great source of confidence to his disciples.

The Church is to be on the way of the Lord with the Lord himself. Though Jesus ascends into heaven, he continues to work with his disciples, confirming their work. With the Lord, risen and enthroned, nothing in heaven nor on earth can ultimately stop the followers of Jesus on the way of the Lord from accomplishing the will of God.

What happens to Jesus will happen to all of the people of God. Death ends nothing; it only opens the door to a further, deeper, fuller experience of the kingdom of God. Acknowledging such truth does not dismiss the severity of death; to be forced by accident, disease or old age to give up our bodies, the only home we have known, is no light matter. Jesus, too, dreaded this dark passage.

The way of the Lord passes through a cross for each of us, but that is not the end of the road. Those of us who continue to walk in this way will one day be "taken up into heaven."

Consider:

14. *What does it mean to you that Jesus "was taken up into heaven and sat down at the right hand of God"?*

15. *What do these verses indicate about Jesus' present activity? In what ways have you known that Jesus works with you and confirms your Christian testimony?*

Group Activities

1. Brainstorm the following question, recording answers on chalkboard, whiteboard or newsprint:
   - What do you think is the strongest proof that Jesus has risen from the dead? Why?

   Then discuss the following:
   - Which of these proofs are convincing to people today?
   - What evidence do people today demand in order to believe in Jesus' resurrection?
   - In what ways are those who refuse to believe "hard of heart"?
   - What is our responsibility toward those who do not believe?

2. Invite group members to share their responses to question 7. Record major ideas on chalkboard, whiteboard or newsprint. Discuss:
   - What suggestions can we make to our community that would help us avoid somber funerals and facilitate an eager expectation of God's intervention?

3. Reread MARK 16:8 aloud. Divide into groups of two or three to discuss:
   - Why does the thought of witnessing or evangelizing generate a feeling of anxiety in many contemporary Christians?
   - What are we afraid of when we hesitate to tell someone the good news?
   - How are our fears like or unlike the women's at the tomb?
   - What are some antidotes to fear?

4. Distribute several newspapers or news magazines. Invite group members to look for evidence of the resurrection, the living presence of the Spirit of Christ. Share these findings with the whole group.

Journal Meditation

Close your eyes and relax for a few moments. Breathe easily. Now imagine that you are looking up into heaven. There you see a huge multitude of people and angels gathered around the throne of God. You look closer. It is hard to see God because there is such a bright light shining from the throne, but you can see Jesus sitting at the right hand of God. You come closer to him and see his face. It is shining with the glow of God's light. God is reflected there. What do you see? What feelings do you have? After searching Jesus' face, write or illustrate below what you hope to see and feel when you are "taken up into heaven."

Stepstone to Prayer

Lord, I see your face. I love you...

Bibliography

Anderson, Janice Capel and Stephen D. Moore, eds. *Mark and Method: New Approaches in Biblical Studies*. Minneapolis: Fortress Press, 1992.

Dowd, Sharyn E. *Reading Mark: A Literary and Theological Commentary on the Second Gospel* (Reading the New Testament Series). Macon, GA: Smyth & Helwys, 2001.

Hooker, Morna D. *The Gospel According to Saint Mark* (Black's New Testament Commentary). Peabody, MA: Hendrickson Publishers, Inc., 1993.

Juel, Donald H. *The Gospel of Mark* (Interpreting Biblical Texts Series). Nashville: Abingdon Press, 1999.

La Verdiere, Eugene. *The Beginning of the Gospel: Introducing the Gospel of Mark*. 2 Volumes. Collegeville: Liturgical Press, 1999.

Malina, Bruce and Richard Rohrbaugh, eds. *Social Science Commentary on the Synoptic Gospels*. Minneapolis: Fortress, 1992.

Meyers, Ched. *Binding the Strong Man: A Political Reading of Mark's Story of Jesus*. Maryknoll, NY: Orbis Books, 1989.

Rhoads, David M., Johanna Dewey, Donald Michie. *Mark as Story: An Introduction to the Narrative of a Gospel*. 2nd ed. Minneapolis: Fortress Press, 1999.

Senior, Donald. *The Passion of Jesus in the Gospel of Mark*. Wilmington, DE: Michael Glazier, 1984 (now available through the Liturgical Press, Collegeville, MN).

Telford, William. *The Theology of the Gospel of Mark* (New Testament Theology Series). Cambridge: Cambridge University Press, 1999.